GOD'S
DAY
TIMER

GOD'S DAY TIMER

MARK BILTZ

 WND Books

GOD'S DAY TIMER

Copyright © 2016 by Mark Biltz

Published by WND Books, Washington, D.C. WND Books is a registered trademark of WorldNetDaily.com, Inc. ("WND")

Book designed by Mark Karis

WND Books are available at special discounts for bulk purchases. WND Books also publishes books in electronic formats. For more information call (541) 474-1776, e-mail orders@ wndbooks.com or visit www.wndbooks.com.

Unless otherwise indicated, Scripture quotations are taken from the American King James Version (public domain).

Hardcover ISBN: 978-1-944229-23-8
eBook ISBN: 978-1-944229-24-5

Library of Congress Cataloging-in-Publication Data
Names: Biltz, Mark, 1956- author.
Title: God's day timer : the believer's guide to divine appointments / Mark
    Biltz.
Description: Washington DC : WND Books, 2016. | Includes bibliographical
    references and index.
Identifiers: LCCN 2016005056 | ISBN 9781944229238 (pbk.)
Subjects: LCSH: God (Christianity)--Eternity. | Time--Religious
    aspects--Christianity. | Providence and government of God--Christianity. |
    Fasts and feasts in the Bible.
Classification: LCC BT153.I47 B55 2016 | DDC 263--dc23
LC record available at https://lccn.loc.gov/2016005056

Printed in the United States of America
17 18 19 20 21 LBM 9 8 7 6 5 4 3 2

To my beloved wife, Vicki, of almost forty years. If it hadn't been for your thinking about me and buying me a book that radically changed my life, this one would never have happened. Your unwavering commitment and love could only be from heaven above.

CONTENTS

INTRODUCTION

It was a beautiful year back in the mid-'90s when Vicki, my beautiful wife of now thirty-nine years, bought me a book that radically changed my life. We had been attending a small church in Buckley, Washington, and I decided I needed a break from church. I had been working a full-time job plus a part-time job to make ends meet. Additionally, I was teaching at the church and serving on the elder board as well. I decided to take a year off and not go anywhere to church, just rest.

During that year off, Vicki, who was passionate about birds, was looking for some good bird books at a bookstore. She knew I was equally passionate about the Bible and my Jewish roots, as I am Jewish on my father's side. We have our ancestry going back to the 1600s. Our last name wasn't always Biltz, but used to be Hirsch. My great, great, great grandfather changed his name from Hirsch to Biltz. Our ancestral town was Mutzig, France. I have Biltz relatives who died in the Holocaust and are listed in Yad Vashem, the Holocaust Museum in Israel.

While browsing, Vicki spied a book by Moshe Braun, called *The Jewish Holy Days: Their Spiritual Significance*, and she bought it for me.

I had gone to Bible college in Wichita back in the '70s and

even studied the feasts of the Lord. The problem is, my training was totally from a replacement-theology perspective, or one that teaches that the church has replaced the Jews as recipients of God's Old Testament promises. For the next twenty-five years I was totally involved in church, teaching, and volunteering, as well as working full-time. Now, during the time off, as I began to read this book, I saw the beauty, the humility, the insights from the Bible as never before; it just took my breath away. It was a fresh way of seeing the Bible through another perspective.

I immediately knew I had to go relearn—and unlearn—a lot of what I had been taught. I still believed then, and do now, all the fundamental truths of Christianity, but now I see those truths in full-color 3-D rather than just black and white. The Bible became alive to me in a new way. I learned how to study the Bible from people who had three thousand years' experience! Why reinvent the wheel?!

Now, understand that religion can be a lot like meat. Take chicken, for example. I know how to eat chicken: I eat the meat and throw out the bone. Sometimes you have to do the same with "religion." Sure, there are bones in Judaism, but there are also a lot of bones in Christianity. Even so, I am not going to turn down a T-bone steak because there's a big bone it! I eat the good, the valuable, and throw out the rest. Of course, you have to be mature enough to have teeth before you can even start eating meat.

Many people from all different denominations tell me they are tired of only getting a spiritual diet of milk and cookies at church, and they are starving for some meat and potatoes. Their "seeker-friendly" churches have completely watered down the gospel and focus only on the new believers, so the more mature congregants never hear anything beyond a salvation message. Others say all their churches teach is positive thinking, with no scriptures, and the leaders just want to be "life coaches," satisfied to know nothing of the Bible. They might give one Bible verse—and then go on for half an hour or more about social issues. Well, my focus is the Word of God. Therefore, I have cited more than 350 scripture references in this book, as I believe you want to know more about what the Lord has to say than what I have to say. All I want to do is connect the dots between the scriptures, that you might stand in awe of what your heavenly Father wants you to see from His heart!

People who come to El Shaddai Ministries or watch for free our live streaming services from around the world all share the same testimony. These are people who have been saved for twenty years or more, yet they all say, "We've been robbed! Why haven't we heard these truths before?" All I can say is people don't know what they don't know. I want to expand their knowledge. I hope to do the same for you.

I am so glad you want to go on this journey with me as we unlock treasure chests full of golden insights regarding God's calendar. What's in store for God's people? What's next on His timeline of events? How do the biblical feasts relate to the future—*our* future? What does God want us to know about them? Do they have any relevance for the church? In the chapters ahead, we'll explore all of these questions.

Now, sit back, put on your 3-D Bible glasses, and come with me on an adventure that will radically change your life.

1

THE BIBLICAL CALENDAR

Are you ready to go on the most thrilling adventure of your life? To me there is nothing more exciting than a treasure hunt—and we're about to embark on one.

God has treasures, hidden for you, all throughout the Bible. According to Proverbs 25:2, He "delights in concealing things" (MSG). Why? Because He wants us to "search them out" (WYC). Sadly, many have abandoned the search and headed back to the entertainment that the world offers. And yet, nothing compares to discovering all the nuggets buried along His ancient paths.

If there is anyone who knows how to have a treasure hunt, it is God Almighty. And He has some really cool treasures to hide. He just wants to see if we are really motivated to continue the search until we find them—or if we will just give up.

Over the last forty years, I have discovered several biblical keys that unlock hidden treasures. There are treasure chests *full* of insight much more precious than gold and silver, so I am compelled to share these keys with you. In the coming pages, I will lay them out for you; then you decide if you want to open the treasure chests for yourself and go on to the greatest adventure of your life.

The first key is this: if you want to understand the Bible,

go to the very beginning of the Bible. The Lord says in Isaiah 46:10 that He declares the end from the beginning. So, if you want to know the end of the book, first find the patterns in the beginning of the book. Ecclesiastes 1:9 tells us that what has been is what will be, and what has been done is what will be done; there is nothing new under the sun. Either we believe God at His Word or we don't. So let's begin at the very beginning, in the book of Genesis.

In Genesis 1:14, God declares that He is creating the sun and the moon for "signs, and for seasons, and for days, and years." When we read this, we naturally think of our calendar, made up of the seasons known as winter, spring, summer, and fall. One of the first major nuggets I uncovered was that the Hebrew word for "seasons," *moed*, does not mean seasons as we know them. That same Hebrew word is translated as "feasts" in Leviticus 23:2. When I think of a feast, I'm thinking of a big turkey dinner. So which is the correct translation for the Hebrew word *moed*? Does it mean "fall" or "food"? Believe it or not, neither one accurately describes the Hebrew word or concept.

The word *moed* is better translated as "divine appointments." God has prescheduled divine encounters with his people, operating on a calendar different from the one the world uses.

When the terms "days" and "years" are used in Genesis 1:14, they're not meant to indicate Monday or Tuesday or the year on our Gregorian calendar. The Bible is actually referring to the timing on God's own, prophetic calendar. The "days" mean holy days, like the new moon and the Sabbath, as well as Passover, Pentecost, and Tabernacles. The term *years* refers to the Jubilee years, which occur every fiftieth year, and the *shemittah* years, which happen every seventh year. (God determined that the nation of Israel was to let the Promised Land rest every seven years, during which there would be an economic reset for His people. Every fiftieth year, all alienated land would return to its original owners.) So in Genesis, God was saying that both the sun and the moon would determine when Israel was to celebrate these divine appointments. Because each of these divine appointments were to be dress rehearsals to the very day and hour on God's calendar when they would find their prophetic fulfillment.

The Islamic calendar is based solely on the moon. It is a very accurate calendar, but not the one God uses. Conversely, most of the world operates on a pagan calendar, started by Julius Caesar and modified by Pope Gregory, that is based solely on the sun. Scientifically it's an extremely accurate calendar, but it's just not the one God uses. In Genesis, God said that both the sun *and* the moon were to be used in determining when the divine appointments should be. This is critical to our understanding of the timing of when God will intersect human history.

If your boss told you to meet him at 4:00 p.m. on Friday and you told him that it wouldn't fit in your schedule, so he'd better change it to 8:00 a.m. on Monday, what would he say? Would you have a job on Monday? What would you say if someone told you that we needed to start keeping the Fourth of July on the fourth of June? How about keeping Thanksgiving in March? You would say they were crazy.

Now, imagine that you are a salesperson, and you have an appointment scheduled with a potential client that could mean the biggest sale ever for your company. A couple of days before, you go to a Starbucks and sit down to have coffee and plan your schedule for the next week. It just so happens that when you leave, your day planner is still on the table. Unbeknownst to you, your competitor is sitting at the table next to you, and as soon as you walk out the door, he changes the appointment time in your day planner so you will be late. Later, when you return to pick it up, you are relieved to see your planner still sitting on the table, but have no idea that it has been tampered with.

On the day of the appointment, your competitor shows up on time and makes the sale—and you come an hour late.

That is exactly what the adversary did with the biblical calendar, so we would miss the divine appointments.

In Daniel 7:24–25, we read about an evil one who would come and think to change the times and laws. This is exactly what happened! From either ignorance or anti-Semitism, the biblical timing of God's divine appointments has been changed, added to, removed, and placed on a pagan calendar that has no correlation to His. I will give you a perfect example.

As a believer in the gospel and in Yeshua, or Jesus, I celebrate the Lord's Passover. I also celebrate the Feast of Firstfruits, when Yeshua rose from the dead. In Christianity it is called Easter. We must remember that Passover was called "the LORD's Passover," not just the Jewish Passover (Ex. 12:11; Lev. 23:5). In the gospel of Luke, Yeshua said that every year when Passover was celebrated, it was to be done in remembrance of Him (22:19). First Corinthians 11:23–26 states that Yeshua commanded us to remember His death. When Yeshua said this He was referring to the Passover Seder that had been celebrated annually for 1,500 years on Nisan 14 as was commanded by God. Now He was saying, when you celebrate Passover every year on the fourteenth day of the first month I want you to realize this was a dress rehearsal of what I was going to accomplish! Denominations never celebrate Passover as Yeshua commanded. What was instituted instead was the concept of communion. But now man's tradition is making the Word of God to none effect just as Yeshua had stated concerning some of the Jewish traditions. Christians do celebrate the Resurrection, but because it is kept according to the pagan calendar rather than the biblical calendar, Easter, or the Resurrection, is often celebrated a month before Yeshua even died. For example, in 2016 Easter fell on Sunday, March 27, but Passover was a month later, on Friday, April 22. How could Christians celebrate His *resurrection* a month before His *crucifixion*?

The biblical injunction that the Lord gave Moses concerning Passover was "Remember this day" (Ex. 13:3). In Luke 22:19, at their last Passover Seder together, Yeshua told His disciples to "do this in remembrance of me." Yet, no longer does Christianity celebrate the biblical holiday of Passover on the day commanded in the Bible, the fourteenth of Nisan (or Abib, as it was called before the Babylonian captivity), the first month of the ecclesiastical year on the Jewish calendar. Constantine, who had no knowledge of the Scriptures, arbitrarily changed the date due to heavy anti-Semitism, or Jew hatred, at the council of Nicea in AD 325.

In Numbers 9, we read about some men who, because they had been defiled by the body of a dead man, couldn't keep the Passover on the day they were supposed to. When Moses asked the Lord what they should do, the Lord told Moses that if anyone was unclean because of a dead body, or was out of town, they could still keep the Passover, but on the fourteenth day of the *second month* (v. 11). We see this actually occurred on a national scale during the time of Hezekiah.

Hezekiah had sent letters to all of Israel and Judah summoning them to the house of the Lord at Jerusalem to keep the Passover. He had taken counsel about keeping the Passover in the second month because the priests hadn't sanctified themselves sufficiently and the people hadn't gathered themselves in time to keep it in the first month (2 Chron. 30:1–3). So, "they killed the Passover lamb on the fourteenth day of the second month" (v. 15), and afterward they also kept other holy days that had been neglected. And what was God's response to the priests? "Their voice was heard, and their prayer came up to his holy dwelling place, even unto heaven" (v. 27). He was pleased with their efforts! So we see from the Scriptures that God approved celebrating Passover in the second month. Who are we to edit His Word?

Now let me ask you something. Are we supposed to do what is convenient, or do what God says? Are we to follow the majority, or God alone? Do we act according to our reason, or according to God's Word? Do we observe what is politically correct, or what is biblically correct? Will we blindly follow our leaders, as Christians did in Hitler's Germany, or should we follow the Bible?

If you think the mention of Hitler is extreme here, look at the following letter, wherein Constantine changed the date of Easter. Also observe *why* the date was changed (remember, too, that the early Gentile leaders had no background in Torah; their entire moral value system came from the ancient Greek philosophy of Socrates, Aristotle, and Plato—pagans all):

> From the Letter of the Emperor [Constantine] to all those not present at the Council. (Found in Eusebius, *Vita Const.*, Lib III 18–20.)

When the question relative to the sacred festival of *Easter*
arose, it was *universally* thought that *it would be convenient*
that all should keep the feast on one day . . . It was declared
to be particularly unworthy for this, the holiest of festivals,
to follow the customs [the calculation] of the Jews who
had soiled their hands with the most fearful of crimes, and
whose minds were blinded. In rejecting their custom, . . .
we may transmit to our descendants the legitimate mode of
celebrating Easter . . . We ought not therefore to have anything in common with the Jew, for the Saviour has shown
us another way; our worship follows a more legitimate and
more convenient course (the order of the days of the week;
and consequently, in unanimously adopting this mode, we
desire, dearest brethren to separate ourselves from the detest-
able company of the Jews, for it is truly shameful for us to
hear them boast that without their direction we could not
keep this feast. How can they be in the right, they who, after
the death of the Saviour, have no longer been led by reason
but by wild violence, as their delusion may urge them? They
do not possess the truth in this Easter question, for in their
blindness and repugnance to all *improvements* they frequently
celebrate *two passovers in the same year*. . . .

We could not imitate those who are openly in error. How,
then, could we follow *these Jews* who are most certainly blinded
by error? for to celebrate a passover twice in one year is totally
inadmissible. But even if this were not so, it would still be your
duty not to tarnish your soul by communication with such
wicked people (the Jews). . . . You should consider not only
that the number of churches in these provinces make *a majority*,
but also that it is right to demand what *our reason* approves,
and that we should have nothing in common with the Jews.[1]

Oh my goodness! Do you sense any anti-Semitism here? I guess they forgot that "the Saviour" Himself was Jewish, a fact Hitler himself denied.[2]

The church leaders had already gotten off track by this time, but here is where we really ran off the rails, by declaring God's Word no longer valid in determining parts of their doctrine. Whether it was due to the lack of scriptural knowledge or simply the result of a bad attitude, either way we need to get back on track!

In Acts 3, after the death and resurrection of Yeshua, Peter is speaking before a crowd. As he accuses them of killing the Messiah, he also acknowledges that he knows they had acted in ignorance, as their rulers also had. But then he goes on to say that they need to repent, that the "times of refreshing" may come "from the presence of the Lord." Then, he promised, they would see the return of the appointed Messiah, Yeshua, "whom the heaven must receive until the time of the restitution of all things" about which God had "spoken by the mouth of all his holy prophets" long ago (vv. 17–21). One of those "things" needing to be restored back to the body of Messiah is the observance of God's calendar!

A second key to unlocking the hidden mysteries of end-time events is recognizing that God's divine appointments are "holy convocations," as stated in Leviticus 23:2. The Hebrew word for "convocations" there is *miqra*, which means "assembly." It refers to people *assembling* together for a stated purpose, at an agreed-upon time.

But there is something else involved that, when I investigated this passage more thoroughly, it totally blew me away. Are you ready for this? Are you sitting down? The Hebrew word also implies that the people would be assembling together for a *dress rehearsal.* Do you get that? They were to meet on specific days at specific times on God's schedule to rehearse what would happen on the very same day in the future.

Why do you think God had Israel slay the Passover lamb every year on Nisan 14? Because that is the very day Yeshua would die! Why do you think He commanded Israel fifteen hundred years before the book of Acts to gather together every year on the Feast of Shavuot—also known as Pentecost—in Jerusalem? Because in Jerusalem, on that very day, the Ruach HaKodesh (Holy Spirit) would be poured out, turning the world upside down.

Do you believe the Lord is the same yesterday, today, and forever? Do you *really* believe it? Is there any doubt? Then this next biblical key will really rock your world!

If He *is* really the same yesterday, today, and forever, then if He fulfilled the spring feasts to the day of His first coming, He will fulfill the fall feasts to the day of His second coming! So, we will first investigate the spring feasts in detail, including how they were fulfilled not only to the day but also to the very hour. Then we will explore the fall feasts to see, prophetically, what will happen on those very days in the future. Please meditate on these last statements very carefully.

Realize that in no way are we setting dates! We have no idea what year anything will happen, but we *can* know the times and seasons! And now we know that the phrase "times and seasons" refers directly to divinely appointed times on God's calendar.

When I ask people if they want to be at the wedding of the Messiah, they all emphatically declare that they do. So why wouldn't they want to be at the dress rehearsal?! It's the same with the coronation of the Messiah. Every year at the appointed time on God's calendar, thousands of people all over the world join the angelic host in rehearsing the Messiah's coming!

God's command in Leviticus 23:2 was for His children to "proclaim" these divine appointments. In Hebrew the root word means "to call out by name those who have been bidden to come to the event."[3] It's to be a personal invitation. We see this developed in Matthew 22, where the king sends forth his servants to call those who were bidden to the wedding, but they wouldn't come! The second time, he tells different servants to call those who were invited to the wedding, saying, "Please come; everything is ready." Amazingly, they made excuses for why they wouldn't come. Finally, He told his servants to go into the highways and invite all they could find, both the bad and the good, to come to the wedding, "and the wedding was furnished with guests" (v. 10).

The story goes on to mention that a certain guest arrived without a wedding garment on, but was instead dressed in strange apparel, so he was punished (vv. 11–13). This parable comes from the book of Zephaniah, where the prophet wrote about "the day of the LORD." God tells the prophet that He has prepared His sacrifice and bid His guests, but He will punish the king's children and all those "clothed with strange apparel" (Zeph. 1:8). We will look at this more later, but in the meantime, it's amazing to me that people do not realize the importance of attending the dress rehearsals to these prophetic events put on by the King of kings! I feel my responsibility in writing this book is to make you aware that this is your open invitation to the greatest wedding event of all time. Be sure and help me invite all your friends by sending them their invitations!

There are many prophecy buffs out there, but if they are not aware of God's prophetic calendar, they are missing the most important key to unlocking what is coming and when it will happen. Let me give you a very important reason, from the Scriptures.

In Zechariah 8:18–19, God lists the dates when the Jewish people fast annually. These fast days, which are observed in the fourth, fifth, seventh, and tenth months, are also days of mourning. But it is prophesied that these *fasts* will, sometime in the future, turn into *feasts*, and days of great rejoicing. It has been over two thousand years, and that has not happened yet. But if we don't know when these fast days occur on our calendar, we will never know when the prophecies have been fulfilled!

If you believe in prophecy but aren't on God's calendar, you're like a ship drifting aimlessly in the ocean without any navigational equipment. So the takeaway from this chapter is this: if you want to have any inkling of what the God of Israel is doing in these last days, you need to realize that He operates on a different calendar from the one the world uses. And He has preset the times for prophetic fulfillments based on that calendar.

His clock is ticking. The months are changing. Are you prepared?

Many significant prophetic events always happen according to God's calendar. This is repeated over and over. Take, for example, the fast days mentioned in Zechariah. Historically, all four of these fast days have to do with the destruction of the Temple by Nebuchadnezzar. Here is an outline of what transpired:

MONTH	HEBREW DATE	MODERN TIMELINE	EVENT
10TH MONTH	10TH OF TEVET	DECEMBER JANUARY	WALLS OF JERUSALEM SURROUNDED
4TH MONTH	17TH OF TAMMUZ	JUNE JULY	WALLS WERE BROKEN THROUGH
5TH MONTH	9TH OF AV	JULY AUG	TEMPLE DESTROYED
7TH MONTH	1ST OF TISHRI	SEPTEMBER OCTOBER	GEDALIAH KILLED

Are these fast days important to believers? I'd have to say they are critical to us from several standpoints!

First, again, these fast days are days of mourning, or weeping, and have been for the last twenty-five hundred years. Rabbi Shaul, whom believers know as the apostle Paul, taught the Roman church to rejoice with those who rejoice and weep with those who weep (Rom. 12:15). In context, this is immediately after a chapter where he was writing about the relationship of the nations to the nation of Israel! We have been grafted or adopted into their family. God did not start a new family.

A couple of chapters later, Paul wrote that whoever regards a certain day as holy regards it to the Lord, and he who does not regard the day, it is to the Lord alone that he does not observe it. Furthermore, he who eats, eats to the Lord and gives thanks, but he who doesn't eat, it is to the Lord that he doesn't; he still gives God thanks (Rom. 14:6). This is simply telling us that whether or not believers from the nations who have joined themselves to Israel want to fast on these days is up to them, but they are encouraged to empathize with Israel.

(This verse has nothing to do with whether or not believers should keep the feasts; it has to do with the fasts.) Either way, they are encouraged in Romans 12:15 to empathize with Israel.

So, let's go back to the significance of the fasts. These were to be annual reminders to repent for the sins that had led to the disasters in the first place. The first one was on the tenth of Tevet. We find in Ezekiel that it was in the ninth year, in the tenth month, on the tenth day of the month, that the word of the Lord came to Ezekiel and told him to write "the name of the day, even of this same day: the king of Babylon set himself against Jerusalem" (Ezek. 24:1–2). If this day was so important to God that He instructed Ezekiel to write it down so it would be recorded forever, then it should be just as important to us.

The fast of the fourth month was on the seventeenth of Tammuz. Look at the pattern here. This was the very day Moses descended from the mountain, saw the golden calf Aaron had made, and broke the first set of tablets containing the Ten Commandments (Ex. 32:19; Mishnah, Taanit 28b). This was also the day the evil king Manasseh, who had built pagan altars for "all the host of heaven in . . . the house of the LORD" (2 Kings 21:5), and had even sacrificed his own children to Molech, set an idol in the holy sanctuary. On that same day, in a different year, the daily offerings had to cease because of the siege by Nebuchadnezzar, and the following year, on that very same day, the walls were breached. The Romans also breached those walls—on the *same* day—in AD 70! In 2 Kings 25:3 we read of the horrible famine that was happening as well.

Did you know that the 2006 Lebanon War also started on the seventeenth of Tammuz in Israel? This was not lost on the Jewish people. This day begins the three weeks of mourning culminating on the next fast day, the ninth of Av.

So what about the ninth of Av? According to Jewish history, it was on that day that the ten spies brought the bad report in fear of the giants.[4] Because of their unbelief, they despised the Promised Land and lifted up their voices and wept. This resulted in a cascade of calamities over the ages. God determined that they would weep every year on this day. It is taught in Jewish history that it was on the ninth of Av when Nebuchadnezzar began to burn the Temple. Unbelievably, this was the very same day that Titus set fire to the Temple in AD 70! In 1290 King Edward of England ordered the expulsion of all the Jews from England on the ninth of Av. The Jewish expulsion from Spain, two centuries later, was also on the ninth of Av. World War I began on that date; Himmler signed the "Final Solution" on that date; then, to top it off, in 2005, Israeli president Ariel Sharon expelled all the Jews from the Gaza Strip at sunset on the ninth of Av! When you are on God's calendar, these biblical dates come alive!

The final fast day from this text is based on the murder of Gedaliah, a governor appointed by Nebuchadnezzar. This is the fast of the seventh month that is commemorated on the third of Tishri, after Rosh Hashanah.[5] Gedaliah had told all the Jews still in Jerusalem to remain there and serve the king of Babylon, and it would be well with them. Instead they assassinated Gedaliah and fled to Egypt (2 Kings 25:22–25), leading to their downfall.

When dates are mentioned in Genesis, such as "the second month, the seventeenth day of the month," which is when the flood of Noah began (7:11), the writer is referring to the time when Tishri was the first month. So the "windows of heaven were opened" on the seventeenth of Cheshvan, roughly mid to late November on our calendar. But from Exodus on, after God told Moses that Nisan was to be the beginning of the religious calendar (Ex. 12:1–2), the second month was Iyar. So where the Bible says that travelers or anyone unclean may celebrate Passover on the fourteenth day of the second month, as in Numbers 9:11, it means the month of Iyar.

Understanding the calendar enables you to see the biblical patterns and recognize God's hands in historical events. Here are some great examples. In Nehemiah 8, after many of God's people had returned from the Babylonian captivity, the people gathered together on "the first day of the seventh month" (v. 2). Now, what jumps out is that this day is Rosh Hashanah! In the book of Esther, after Haman had determined to kill all the Jews, the king's scribes were called to the palace on the thirteenth day of the first month (3:12). They were then sent with the official letter to all the provinces to murder all Jews both young and old, little children and women, in one day. Now we know these letters were dispatched at Passover during the whole week of Unleavened Bread. When Esther heard of it, on Passover, she fasted for three days and three nights (Esth. 4:15–17). On the third day she rose to appear before the king. Can you see the similarities between this story and the account of the Messiah who was in the earth for three days and three nights and rose on the third day during Passover week?

In Daniel 10, we find the prophet fasting for three weeks (vv. 1–3). Then, on the twenty-fourth day of the first month, he had a vision of a man clothed in linen, with a belt of fine gold, a face like lightning, eyes like fire, and a voice like that of a multitude. When this man—an angel—spoke, Daniel fell on his face, but the angel lifted him up and told him not to be afraid (vv. 5–12). Daniel also was fasting during Passover week, and his vision occurred right after Passover week! Tell me if this doesn't sound exactly like what John saw in the book of Revelation, after which he, too, was told not to be afraid (Rev. 1:12–18)!

We also learn from Daniel that the angel would have come sooner, but the prince of Persia prevented him from coming until Michael, God's high angel, helped him. The angel Daniel encountered was trying to warn him of what would befall his people in the end time. Once he did, the angel said, he would have to go back and fight against the prince of Persia again (Dan. 10:13–22)! Since what happens in the heavenlies also tends to happen on earth, could this mean that sometime around Passover there could be a future war between Israel and Persia, or Iran? Certainly, but if we are on the wrong calendar, we will never see the connection!

Following is a chart showing some of the biblical holidays over the next few years and where they fall on our calendar:

YEAR	PASSOVER	TRUMPETS	YOM KIPPUR	SUKKOT	CHANUKAH	PURIM
2016	APR 23	OCT 3	OCT 12	OCT 17	DEC 25	MAR 24
2017	APR 11	SEPT 21	SEPT 30	OCT 5	DEC 13	MAR 12
2018	MAR 31	SEPT 10	SEPT 19	SEPT 24	DEC 3	MAR 1
2019	APR 20	SEPT 30	OCT 9	OCT 14	DEC 23	MAR 21
2020	APR 9	SEPT 19	SEPT 28	OCT 3	DEC 11	MAR 10

This chart compares the order of religious/civil months to our calendar:

RELIGIOUS CALENDAR	MONTH	CIVIL CALENDAR	FEAST	CORRESPONDING MONTHS
1	NISAN	7	PASSOVER/UNLEAVENED BREAD FIRSTFRUITS	MARCH / APRIL
2	IYAR	8		APRIL / MAY
3	SIVAN	9	SHAVUOT	MAY / JUNE
4	TAMMUZ	10		JUNE / JULY
5	AV	11		JULY / AUGUST
6	ELUL	12		AUGUST / SEPTEMBER
7	TISHRI	1	ROSH HASHANAH YOM KIPPUR SUKKOT	SEPTEMBER / OCTOBER
8	CHESHVAN	2		OCTOBER / NOVEMBER
9	KISLEV	3	HANUKKAH	NOVEMBER / DECEMBER
10	TEVET	4		DECEMBER / JANUARY
11	SHEVAT	5		JANUARY / FEBRUARY
12	ADAR	6	PURIM	FEBRUARY / MARCH

Here we see the significance of the individual feasts:

FEAST	TIMES & SEASONS	SIGNIFICANCE
PASSOVER	NISAN 14 SPRING	OUR INDIVIDUAL REDEMPTION
UNLEAVENED BREAD	NISAN 15–21 SPRING	MESSIAH'S BODY WITHOUT SIN OR DECAY
FIRSTFRUITS	NISAN SPRING	RESURRECTION OF THE MESSIAH
SHAVOUT / PENTECOST SPIRIT	SIVAN SPRING	GIFTS SENT FROM HEAVEN, BOTH THE TORAH AND THE HOLY SPIRIT
TRUMPETS	TISHRI 1 FALL	JUDGMENT OF THE WORLD BEGINS
YOM KIPPUR	TISHRI 10 FALL	ISRAEL'S NATIONAL DAY OF ATONEMENT
TABERNACLES	TISHRI 15 FALL	MESSIAH'S REIGN, WHEN HE TABERNACLES AMONG US

God carefully planned every one of these divine appointments from the foundation of the world. Before He started the time clock for humanity, God knew what His purposes were for humankind. He is not just some distant, all-knowing being either. He is personally involved with the affairs of this world. It really increases my faith when I see the hand of God in the divine appointments. As I observe His order, and the patterns being repeated, I recognize that there must be a much higher intelligence than man at the helm of human history.

2

PASSOVER: THE LAMB SLAIN FROM THE FOUNDATION OF THE WORLD

Let's continue our treasure hunt by looking at the spring feasts and how God planned them in great detail way in advance. The Bible says, in Revelation 13:8, that the Lamb was "slain from the foundation of the world." This means that the slaying of the Messiah was preplanned from the time of creation. Yeshua's death did not come as a surprise to the Father; He'd *already* planned to resurrect Him!

Imagine, just imagine, if you knew your child was going to die: how much planning would you put into it? God is in complete control, and believe me: when it came to planning His Son's funeral, He put His whole being into it! God determined, way in advance, precisely what day His Son would die. And not only to the day, but to the very hour. As Master Conductor, He planned every detail for the entire memorial service, even determining, a thousand years earlier, what songs would be sung! That's right. A millennium before Yeshua's death, God inspired King David to write the words and the music to the very songs that were to be sung on that fateful day!

We need to begin with an understanding of the biblical calendar system. There are biblical calendars on the Internet that you can download for free that display the Jewish calendar with the one the world uses within the same calendar.[1] There is a civil calendar that is calculated from the time of creation, beginning on the first of Tishri, which falls around September on the secular calendar. Later, God instituted a religious calendar to determine the cycle of the *moedim*, or divine appointments (Ex. 12:2).

Beginning in Numbers 9, we see that Israel was to keep the Lord's Passover in the springtime, on the fourteenth day of Nisan, which is late March or early April on our calendar (vv. 1–5). Nisan was to be the first month of the religious cycle, whereas Tishri is the first month of the civil calendar. But notice the Bible doesn't go into all the ceremonial details of Passover, so we need some background from Jewish history or else we won't have any idea of the rites involved.

Our story kicks off in Egypt over thirty-five hundred years ago, where God told Moses it was time to head to the Promised Land! First, He had some unfinished business to attend to: rendering justice for the wrongs that had been done to Israel. God knew that for Israel to move on, they needed to realize that justice *would* be done to the perpetrators. Many people do not realize that each of the ten plagues was actually aimed at one of the gods of Egypt. But the Lord did say He would execute judgment against all the gods of Egypt (Ex. 12:12). Pharaoh thought that *he* was a god, so he had to be put in his place.

The epic battle began with Moses and Aaron coming before Pharaoh, doing some magic tricks, as far as he was concerned, so he would release the Hebrew slaves. To prove they meant business, Aaron threw down his staff—and it became a crocodile![2]

Pharaoh was not happy . . . but that was only the beginning.

The first god taken down was the Nile god, Hapi. The river turned to blood, symbolizing the death of this false deity. Next came the plague of frogs. The Egyptians worshipped a frog goddess named Heqet. God figured if they liked frogs, He'd give them frogs till they were coming out their ears! Then, it was death to all the frogs. The third god toppled was Geb, god of earth. God turned "earth," or the dust, into lice.

The next plague was against the god of the atmosphere, named Shu. Since this god symbolized air, God filled the air with flying insects. After that He plagued the cattle, to take aim at the bull god Apis, who was proclaimed to be god incarnate.

Heka was the Egyptians' god of magic and medicine, who was believed to carry the tools of a healer. To destroy the people's confidence in that god, God brought boils to everyone, in effect saying, "Heal this!"

The next god shown up by God was the god of the firmament. Talk about a crazy name: his name was Nut! It was Nut's job to protect man from the heavens. So naturally, God brought a plague of hailstones, to show the incompetence of that god. This was followed by a swarm of locusts to disgrace Anubis, god of the fields. Perhaps you have heard of the sun god, Ra. To shame this Egyptian deity, God "knocked his lights out"—by covering the land in darkness for three days.

Lastly, God brought death to all the firstborn, of both man and beast. This was a direct hit on the god known as Amon-Ra, who was believed to be the creator of man. This god was symbolized by a ram, so it should come as no surprise that God told Israel to put the blood of lambs on their doorposts if they wanted to survive this final plague. According to the Egyptian zodiac, the first month of spring, which now also happens to be the first month for the Jews, was the chief month of this god. The constellation Aries, the Latin word for *ram* in ancient Egyptian astronomy, was associated with the god Amon-Ra. Because Aries was the location of the vernal equinox, it was called the "Indicator of the Reborn sun."[3] Now imagine how the Israelites must have felt, living as slaves in Egypt, when God instructed them to have a national cookout and barbecue the Egyptian lamb god outside, so all of Egypt would see Israel eating their god for lunch! You know when your neighbor is cooking up a barbecue! Everyone can smell it. God also told Israel to be sure and put the blood on the outside of the house, so the Egyptians would see that Hebrew slaves outranked an Egyptian god. Talk about politically incorrect! To top it off, this happened at the vernal equinox at the full moon in the constellation Aries, when the Egyptian god is supposed to be at the apex of his strength! Yet God took him down! From a believer's point of view, God was telling the world that the Egyptian god is a fake as He has the true lamb slain for the redemption of Israel. By putting the blood of the lamb, which Egypt worshipped, on the outside of their doors, the Israelites were making a statement: *Paganism and idolatry stop here!*

Now, allow me to sidetrack for a moment to show you something incredible. When God told Moses to use the rod in his hand for "signs" (Ex. 4:17), He used the three-letter word *owt*, in Hebrew spelled אות. Going from right to left, you have the Hebrew letters *aleph*, *vav*, and *tav*. *Aleph* and *tav* are the first and last letters of the Hebrew alphabet. Interestingly, the term "Alpha and Omega," also the first and last letters of the Greek alphabet, is used multiple times for Yeshua, who Himself claimed to be the first and the last (Rev. 1:11, 17; 2:8; 22:13). There can only be one first and one last!

In Isaiah the God of Israel calls Himself the first and the last (41:4; 44:6; 48:12). In Hebrew, rather than saying "Alpha and Omega," it would be the *Aleph Tav*, or את, the Beginning and the End, which represents God. Amazingly, it is this same Aleph Tav whom John saw in the midst of the seven golden candlesticks, with eyes as flames of fire (Rev. 1:12–14). The את spoke to him saying, "I am the First and the Last. I am He who lives, and was dead, and, behold, I am alive forevermore" (vv. 17–18 NKJV). It was the Aleph Tav who died and rose from the dead!

Now, why is this important? Remember that the Hebrew word for "sign" used in Exodus 4 is made up of the letters *aleph* and *tav*, with the letter *vav* in the middle: אות. In the Exodus story, the blood on the doorpost was to be for a "sign" on the Israelites' houses (Ex. 12:13 NKJV). When God saw the blood, He would pass over it, and the plague would not come to their house. Well, in Hebrew, this word for *sign*, while pronounced the same, is spelled differently. An anomaly! Here it is not spelled *aleph-vav-tav*. On this one occasion, in the Passover story, it is just spelled *aleph-tav*, or את! I see this sign as implying that it is the blood of the Aleph Tav that will bring the future redemption of God's people! As it says in Revelation 12:11, "they overcame . . . by the blood of the Lamb"!

Back to Exodus now, the story goes on to say that Israel was to take their lamb, a male of the first year and without blemish, on the tenth day of the first month, Nisan, and hold it for four days, until Passover. Then, in the evening, they were to slay it and eat it that night. It was called the Lord's Passover. They were also commanded to eat unleavened bread for seven days and to observe the Passover sacrifice as an ordinance forever.

In Numbers 9:3, Israel was commanded to keep the Passover on the fourteenth day of Nisan, "according to all its rites and ceremonies." The problem is, the text doesn't mention any! This is where we go to Jewish history to find the missing details.

One of the rites of Passover that has been handed down for thousands of years is the removing of leaven from the house during the Feast of Unleavened Bread. This is actually where the whole concept of spring cleaning comes from. In Deuteronomy 6:7, Israel is commanded to teach their children the commands of the Lord. So, to aid in learning—and to make this fun for the children back in the day—after mom and dad had removed all the leaven from the house, they would hide a little leaven for the children to find. Dad would light a candle, and then the fun search for leaven would begin!

When the children would spot the leaven, they would gleefully point it out to their father. Father would tell the children not to touch it, but to instead allow him to remove it. He would then take a feather and gently sweep the leaven onto a wooden spoon. Next he would wrap the wooden spoon with the leaven into a linen cloth and take it outside of the house to a communal burning place with all the other neighbors' leaven.

The candle the father used is representative of God's Word, as seen in Psalm 119:105: "Your word is a lamp to my feet, and a light to my path." The feather symbolizes the Ruach HaKodesh, or Holy Spirit, whom we see in Psalm 91:4: "He shall cover you with his feathers." The leaven represents sin that needs to be removed. We know Messiah took our sin, or leaven, upon Himself (2 Cor. 5:21). What I find incredible is that when it comes to the leaven in our "houses" or lives, just like the Hebrew fathers of old, our heavenly Father also says to let Him remove it! He takes the feather, the Holy Spirit, and gently places our leaven upon the wooden spoon, representing the cross made of wood. Then it is wrapped in linen, just as Messiah was, and taken outside to become a sacrificial offering (Mark 15:46; Heb. 13:13).

Though ancient Hebrew children were instructed not to touch the leaven they found, it was important for them to participate in the removal of leaven from their house at Passover. In John 2, when Yeshua overturned all the tables of the moneychangers doing business in the Temple—also at Passover—Yeshua was helping His Father remove the leaven from His house in preparation for the Feast of Unleavened Bread (vv. 13–15). The apostle Paul reminds us, too, to "purge out" the leaven when we keep this feast each year (1 Cor. 5:7–8).

Remember that the Passover lamb was to be without blemish and was to be taken on the tenth day of the first month and held for four days. In the meantime, it would be kept safe so that no fault could be found with it. Well, talk about a divine dress rehearsal! Look what we find in the Scriptures concerning Messiah.

In John 12:1 we learn that six days before Passover, Yeshua went to visit Lazarus in Bethany. If Passover is on the fourteenth, then six days earlier would be the eighth. The next day, Yeshua headed to Jerusalem. This was now the ninth day, going into the tenth, when the lambs are brought into Jerusalem to be inspected for four days. It was the tenth of Nisan, the day Israel was to select their Passover Lamb!

As Yeshua was coming from Bethany, over the Mount of Olives and through the Eastern Gate, into the Temple, a great crowd took palm branches and went out to meet Him. They were crying out, "Hosanna! Blessed is He who comes in the name of the LORD!" (John 12:13 NKJV). These words are from Psalm 118:26. Every Passover, hymns from Psalms 113–18, known as the Hallel, are sung at specific times. These particular words were actually being sung to the Passover lambs being led through the Sheep Gate on the north side of the Temple by a large crowd. Trouble arose when this second large crowd began singing the same song to Yeshua as He was being led through the Eastern Gate at the very same time!

After the Passover lambs are selected, there is a four-day inspection of the lambs. What do we find but that Yeshua was inspected over the next four days as well! The Pharisees inspected him, as did the Herodians, the chief priests, the elders, all the council, Pilate, Herod, and even one crucified beside Him—and could find no fault in Him (Mark 12:13; Matt. 26:59–60; Luke 23:13–15, 39–41). The Lamb was found to be without blemish!

Interestingly, at the Last Supper, Yeshua's last Passover Seder, He and His disciples sang a hymn before going out to the Mount of Olives (Matt. 26:30). I know the words to the song they sang! Would you like to know? They were singing from the Hallel! Psalm 118 would have been their final song before departing for the mountain. So what were some of those fateful words being sung just before He was betrayed and rejected? "The stone which the builders rejected has become the chief cornerstone. This was the LORD's doing; it is marvelous in our eyes!" (vv. 22–23 NKJV). Can you believe the detail? Follow with me as we unpack this truly marvelous trail.

When the Roman soldiers crucified Jesus, it was the third hour of the day (Mark 15:24–25). That is nine in the morning, the time of the morning sacrifice. According to Josephus, there were 2,700,200 people at Passover during the time of Yeshua.[4] Imagine a choir made up of over 2 million people, all singing Psalm 118 at the time of the morning sacrifice when Yeshua is being bound to the cross. It was at this time when the priest would bind the Passover lamb to the horns of the altar, to be slain that afternoon. What choreography! Only the Master Conductor could arrange such a masterpiece! Having King David write the songs to be sung at Messiah's death over a thousand years in advance! At the very moment they were binding the lamb to the altar, they were binding Yeshua to the cross as the people sang, "God is the LORD, which has showed us light: bind the sacrifice with cords, even to the horns of the altar" (Ps. 118:27).

Then, as Messiah was being lifted up on the cross, what words was He hearing the people sing? "The Lord is my strength and song; he has become my salvation." We know that Yeshua *means* "salvation." They went on, "The right hand of the Lord is lifted up" (Ps. 118:14, 16 BBE). Isn't this just incredible! The Messiah is being "lifted up" from the earth as the multitudes surrounding the hillside are singing, "The right hand of the Lord is [being] lifted up!" Then, on top of that, Yeshua died at 3 p.m., which is precisely the time of the evening sacrifice and the slaying of the final Passover lamb. The timing of all of these dramatic events could only have been orchestrated by the hand of a God in complete control of human events! Do you see why connecting back to the Jewish roots of the faith ignites a passion for God like never before? It deepens our faith in the God of Abraham, Isaac, and Israel.

With over two million people at Passover, how many lambs had to die to feed them all? It was said that there was to be one lamb for every ten people, so more than 250,000 lambs had to be killed in one day![5] Imagine all the blood being poured out at the base of the Temple altar! If a lamb has just one quart of blood to drain out, that's over 60,000 gallons of blood. Where would all this blood go?

Under the Temple Mount was an underground sewer system that headed south downhill through the Dung Gate into the Hinnom valley. There were also gigantic cisterns of water that could be released to flush things out into the valley of blood. The Hinnom valley was the garbage dump. Imagine with me for a moment the size of the river of the thousands of gallons of blood and water rushing out from the right side of the Temple Mount as the Passover lambs were being slain. The Temple faced east, so the valley of blood is south, or to the right. John 19:34 states that a soldier pierced Yeshua's side, and blood and water poured forth. Isn't it amazing that as the blood and water was pouring forth from the side of the Son of God, a river of blood and water was flowing from the Father's right side as He was in the Holy of Holies?

There is a Jewish mourning ritual called *keriah*, or the rending of garments. It is the most striking expression of grief. We see this portrayed in the story of Joseph, when Reuben discovered that his brother had been sold, and Jacob thought he had died when he saw Joseph's coat of many colors stained with blood (Gen. 37:29–34). David also rent his garment when he heard of Saul's death (2 Sam. 1:11). Job rent his garment at the news of the death of his children (Job 1:20). *Keriah* allowed those mourning to give expression to their pent-up anguish in a religiously sanctioned way.

The rending of the veil of the Temple from top to bottom was the Father expressing His deep anguish over the death of His Son (Matt. 27:51)!

What I look for when I'm studying God's Word is patterns. Learning how to study the Bible text from a Jewish perspective, using their methodology, has really opened my eyes to insights I had never seen before. To me, it is like having a thousand-piece puzzle. The Jews have half of the pieces, and Christianity has half of the pieces, but neither has the box top to know what the whole picture is supposed to look like. There are pieces that are very difficult to understand and don't seem to fit with the other pieces we have. Not until we all rise above our pride, arrogance, and animosity on both sides, thinking we alone have all the pieces of the puzzle, will we solve it.

Here is an example of looking at a New Testament text with an understanding of the Hebraic way of studying by looking for patterns. In the gospel of Mark we read about Yeshua entering a synagogue on the Sabbath and seeing a man with a withered hand (3:1–6). The Pharisees were watching Yeshua to see if He would heal the man on the Sabbath so they could accuse Him of breaking the Torah. There were actually several categories of Pharisees, and they did not all hold to the same teachings. Some Pharisees believed you could heal on the Sabbath; others thought you couldn't. The Greek word for "accuse" in the text is the word from which we get our word *categorize*. So they were trying to accuse Him *and* categorize Him.

Yeshua told the man with the withered hand to come to

Him. He then asked the people, "Is it lawful to do good on the sabbath days, or to do evil? to save life, or to kill?" They responded with complete silence and a deer-in-the-headlights look on their faces. Grieved at the hardness of their hearts, Yeshua commanded the man, "Stretch out your hand!" (v. 5 NKJV). The man obeyed, and instantly his hand was healed.

The Pharisees went out and immediately held counsel with the Herodians to see how they might destroy Him.

One might conclude that these guys were acting totally over-the-top in wanting to kill Yeshua for simply healing someone. If I disagree with someone doctrinally, I'm not going to go out and confer with others on how to kill him. But something much deeper was happening here. Maybe it wasn't because of what Yeshua did that day, but because of what He said. The Pharisees had wanted to categorize *Him* and put *Him* in a box. Instead He put *them* in a box so tight theologically, in front of everyone else, that it was game over! Yeshua didn't have *time* to play games, so He just threw them to the mat and pinned them so fast they were furious!

The handicapped man didn't ask to be healed; he was just there. But Yeshua turned his handicap into a teaching opportunity. After all, that's what's supposed to happen in the synagogue on the Sabbath. The Pharisees were trying to catch Yeshua in a "Moses trap." Little did they realize that *He* was the one who told Moses what to write! So Yeshua was saying, "If you want to go there, let's go there—but you are the ones who are going to be caught!"

There are two very well-known Old Testament passages that the Pharisees would have known by heart. The first was Deuteronomy 11:26-28, where Moses told the people that he was setting before them a blessing if they obeyed the Lord's commandments, and a curse if they did not. The second was Deuteronomy 30:15–18, where Moses set before them "life and good, and death and evil." We always have a choice to make. Moses told them that if they would love the Lord, walk in His ways, and keep His statutes and ordinances, then they would live and multiply, and the Lord would bless them! But if their hearts turned away, they would perish.

So now we see Yeshua reenacting Moses for the Pharisees. It's as though He was saying, "Okay, guys, so Moses' law prohibits certain things on the Sabbath. Yet, here we are, celebrating the Sabbath, and we have someone who needs healing. Well, I'm putting before you a choice, just as Moses did: a blessing if you obey, and a curse if you disobey. Obeying means pursuing life and good, and disobeying means pursuing death and evil. So are you *really* observing the Sabbath according to Moses? If you are, you will certainly want Me to choose life and good. If you are not, then who are you to accuse *Me* of disobeying the law of Moses?"

As you can imagine, this was a very annoying line of questioning for the Pharisees. They were not expecting to have Moses reenacted with this radical reinterpretation. When faced with this kind of choice, would you want to say, "I will obey the commandments—which means not choosing life and blessing, but evil"? Well, they knew exactly what He was saying, and now they were totally paralyzed. They had *hoped* to use Moses against Him, but instead, His questions implied that the real Moses was against them and their perception. How did they respond? Total silence. And we are told that He looked around at them with anger, grieved at their *hardness of heart*.

Anyone acquainted with the Hebrew Scriptures knows there was one person above all others who suffered from hardness of heart: Pharaoh of Egypt. God had told Pharaoh, through Moses, "Let my people go," but every time Pharaoh was about to do just that, he hardened his heart. Instead of showing compassion, he kept the people in bondage.

Yeshua, who had just correctly interpreted Moses for the Pharisees, now went a step further. He played the role of YHVH, looking at the hard-hearted Pharisees as though they were the Pharaoh who would not "let His people go." The man with the withered hand had become a stand-in for the people of Israel in bondage to Egypt. So Yeshua said to the man, "Stretch out your hand."

In the Exodus story we continually hear of God stretching forth His hand (Ex. 3:20; 6:6; 7:5; 9:15). God also told Moses, "Stretch out your hand" multiple times in bringing the plagues upon Egypt (e.g., 7:19; 8:5; 9:22). The culmination in bringing salvation and redemption to Israel was when YHVH told Moses to "stretch out" his hand over the sea. I love the connections here! First YHVH told Moses to stretch out his hand to divide the sea, so the children of Israel could go through the midst of it on dry ground. Then YHVH said, "I will harden the hearts of the Egyptians [so] they shall follow them" into the sea (Ex. 14:17). The next time Moses "stretched forth his hand," the Egyptians were drowned when the "sea returned to [its] strength" (v. 27)—*just as the man's withered hand returned to its strength*. Remember that this all happened right after the first Passover.

The Passover story is so central to every Jew, and it was as familiar to Yeshua's listeners in the synagogue as the Sermon on the Mount is to Christians. Surely they could see the connection between Pharaoh's hard-heartedness and their own. They also knew that Yeshua was implying that they were denying the handicapped man "life and good." No wonder they were so mad.

But here is what *really* blew a vein in their necks: In Leviticus 23 we read that the Feast of Unleavened Bread is a seven-day feast. The first day is a Sabbath and the last day is a Sabbath. It has always been taught that the day the children of Israel crossed the Red Sea on the last day of the feast. So here, as the Pharisees were challenging Yeshua with the law of Moses, Yeshua was reminding them that even Moses stretched forth his hand on the Sabbath! What's more, the stretching out of Moses' hand on the Sabbath brought both deliverance and judgment: deliverance to those who obeyed God; judgment to those who did not! Similarly, in Yeshua's reenactment, the same hand brought both deliverance and judgment. As the man stretched forth his withered hand, he brought life—deliverance—to himself, but judgment on the Pharisees.

Yeshua had just thrown a bombshell in the midst of His listeners. He had shown them they had created a Moses in their own image. They were following a faux Moses, not the real Moses, who did life-giving work on the Sabbath, as directed by God Himself! This so challenged their belief system that they were ready to kill over it.

How might this story challenge our own response when our image of Yeshua is also radically altered? So many people have created a God in their own image rather than realizing that they were created in His! This is why we have a black Jesus, a Chinese Jesus, a Hispanic Jesus, and even a white European Jesus with blond hair and blue eyes! Will anger rise up within us when we are challenged by a real Yeshua who differs from our perception of the faux Jesuses we've created in our own image?

There is so much to be seen as we go deeper into the roots of our faith. So let's continue our journey into Passover week and move on to the rest of the spring feasts.

3

FEAST OF UNLEAVENED
BREAD TO PENTECOST

In Leviticus 23:6–8 we learn that after Passover, which ends on the fourteenth of Nisan, comes the Feast of Unleavened Bread, starting on the fifteenth. The Israelites were to eat unleavened bread for seven days. The first day of the Feast of Unleavened Bread is considered a Sabbath day even if it falls during the week. Many get confused into thinking Yeshua died on a Friday because in John 19:31 it mentions the following day was the Sabbath. It wasn't referring to the Saturday Sabbath but instead to the first day of the feast, on the fifteenth of Nisan. According to Leviticus, both the first day and the last day were considered Sabbaths: "In the first day . . . you shall do no servile work therein. . . . In the seventh day . . . you shall do no servile work therein" (Lev. 23:7–8). So in a two-week time period you can have four Sabbaths.

In Numbers 33:3–4 we read that it was on the fifteenth of Nisan that all the Egyptians buried their firstborn that had perished that day. I find it fascinating that Yeshua, who was a firstborn, was also buried on the first day of unleavened bread. We know from the Scriptures that leaven speaks of sin. The seven days of unleavened bread and the eating of matzah are to be a reminder that Messiah was without sin, as declared in Isaiah 53:9: "He had done no violence, neither was any deceit in his mouth." We eat matzah to remember our need to incorporate His sinless life into our life.

During this week Israel also celebrated the Feast of Firstfruits, specifically, the firstfruits of the barley harvest. Israel was to bring a sheaf of their harvest to the priest, and he would wave it before the Lord on the morrow after the Sabbath (Lev. 23:10–11). The big debate back then, and it even continues today, more than three thousand years later, is, which Sabbath day was the writer referring to? Was he referring to the Saturday Sabbath, or to the Sabbath that falls on Nisan 15, the first day of the Feast of Unleavened Bread? I am of the opinion that verse 11 refers to the Saturday Sabbath. Therefore, most likely Yeshua rose from the dead sometime after sunset on Saturday night. This way He rose from the dead on the first day of the week, becoming the firstfruits of the resurrection. Indeed, Mark 16:2 tells us that "very early in the morning the first day of the week," the women came to the tomb and found it empty.

In John 12:24, Yeshua had mentioned that if a kernel of grain falls into the ground and dies, it will bring forth much fruit. In Colossians 1:18 we see that Messiah was that very grain that died, was buried, and then rose from the dead, becoming that sheaf of firstfruits (1 Cor. 15:20)! That very morning, through the time of the morning sacrifice, thousands were bringing their sheaf of firstfruits, the best of their crops, to the priest and waved it before the Lord. And that very same morning, Yeshua, after speaking to Mary outside the tomb (John 20:11–18), ascended, stood before His Father, and presented Himself as the Firstfruits of the Resurrection on the Feast of Firstfruits! The timing again is just so incredible! At the same moment the high priest was waving the sheaf of the firstfruits in the earthly Temple, Yeshua was in the heavenly temple, waving hello to the Father. Everything the earthly priests had ever done was a divine dress rehearsal for the real event, which would be prophetically fulfilled to the very day on God's calendar.

Because the Church is not using the biblical calendar, but one started by pagan Rome, we find Easter is celebrated an entire month before Passover four times just over a twenty-year time period in 2016, 2024, 2027, and 2035! We have a major decision to make as believers. Are we going to obey God or man? Will we celebrate the resurrection of Jesus on God's calendar or throw Him in with the Easter bunny on the pagan calendar?

Back in our main text in Leviticus 23, we discover that God's people were to count from the "morrow after the Sabbath" fifty days until the next divine appointment on God's calendar (vv. 15–17). So beginning from the first day of the Feast of Firstfruits, they counted fifty days to the Feast of Shavuot, also known biblically as the Feast of Weeks, because they counted seven weeks until the fiftieth day (Deut. 16:16). Christians know it as the Feast of Pentecost, but what's funny is that many Christians have no idea that the Jewish people had already been keeping the Feast of Pentecost for fifteen hundred years before the event we read about in the book of Acts. Even two thousand years beyond the New Testament event, the Jews, to this day, still celebrate it.

The Feast of Shavuot was also known as the Feast of Harvest, when the firstfruits of the wheat crop were brought in. All of these feasts or divine appointments were to be visual insights into what God would do prophetically. This is why in the Gospels, Yeshua used metaphors such as "the harvest . . . is great, but the laborers are few" (Luke 10:2 NKJV). He was obviously talking about people being harvested into the kingdom. The fifty-day count was known biblically as the "Counting of the Omer," the Omer being the sheaf of firstfruits that was brought into the Temple. Yeshua ascended to heaven from the Mount of Olives on the fortieth day of the Counting of the Omer. All of the reappearances of Yeshua were during the Counting of the Omer.

Now, let's go for a moment to the book of Acts. In Acts 2 we read that devout Jews from every nation under heaven were gathered in Jerusalem "in one place" (vv. 1, 5). That "place" was the holy Temple itself, not some upper room, as is believed. Why were there Jews from every nation there? Because they were commanded to be there! Notice that Acts 2:5 doesn't say that "pagan gentiles" were there. It says "devout Jews" (NET). The Spirit wasn't poured out on unsuspecting pagans fornicating in their pagan temples. He was poured out on devout Jews who were worshipping God according to His commands on the day He decreed at the location He required. The text goes on to say that the Spirit was poured out at the third hour of the day (v. 15), or 9:00 a.m. That is the time of the morning sacrifice! Another unbelievable dress rehearsal on the appointed day! And three thousand Jews became messianic (v. 41)! Then, a little later, another five thousand Jews believed in the Messiah (Acts 4:4)! Later we even see that there were tens of thousands of Jews who believed and were still zealous for the Torah (Acts 21:20)! Even a great company of the priests believed in Yeshua as the Messiah (Acts 6:7). Talk about a harvest during the Feast of Harvest!

To the Jewish people the Feast of Shavuot, or Pentecost, is a celebration of the giving of the Torah on Mount Sinai thirty-five hundred years ago. On that day, fire fell from heaven, God spoke to His people, and Moses headed up the mount to receive the Ten Words written on the stone tablets. Every year for this feast, the Jews have set readings from the Bible. They read Exodus 19–20 because this is the recorded history of the event. So in Acts 2, the disciples had been up all night reading about God descending in fire. They also read and discussed the first chapter of Ezekiel, which talks about the glory of the Lord appearing, flashes of lightning, and coals of fire. The other passage the disciples were studying was Ezekiel 3, where Ezekiel wrote of the Spirit lifting him up as he heard "a voice of great rushing." Twice he mentioned this noise of a great rushing (vv. 12, 13). So while these Jewish men were contemplating these very verses, along comes a rushing mighty wind! Coincidence?

By the way, the disciples also read the book of Ruth, about a gentile woman being grafted into Israel and who worked the harvest from Passover to Shavuot, or the barley harvest to the wheat harvest (Ruth 2:23). So the spring feasts were fulfilled not only to the day but also to the very hour!

You may recall the story from Acts 3 where Peter and John went up to the temple to pray at the ninth hour and healed a man who had been lame from birth (vv. 1–6). Here is an example of a missing link due to our being cut off from our Jewish roots. Our English translation of verse 1 is wrong. Where it says, "the hour of prayer," it actually should say "the hour of *the* prayer." Which prayer? I can tell you!

In Daniel 6:10 we are told that Daniel prayed three times a day. In the fifth century before Christ, the 120 men of the great assembly composed the basic text of a prayer known as the *Amidah*. This is translated to mean "the Standing Prayer."

Everyone stands when this prayer is recited. The Amidah is the central prayer of the daily services, being recited four times a day: in the morning, afternoon, evening, and one additional time. At a minimum there was an obligation to pray three times a day.

Realize that in Yeshua's time this prayer was already twice as old as the United States is now. It was ingrained in Jewish culture by then, having been recited four times daily for centuries. This is the prayer they were saying in Acts 3 at the time of the evening sacrifice! The Standing Prayer consists of eighteen blessings to the God of Israel. One of the blessings is also a prayer for healing. It goes like this:

Heal us O LORD, and we will be healed;

save us and we will be saved, for you are our praise.

O grant a perfect healing to all our ailments,

for you, almighty King are a faithful and merciful healer.

Blessed are you, O Lord, the healer of the sick of his people Israel.

Every Jew wants to be standing for the Standing Prayer. This man in Acts had been praying to be healed four times a day for close to forty years (Acts 4:22), and he, too, wanted to be standing for the Standing Prayer! And it was at this very moment, during this very prayer, that Peter pulled him up! And immediately his feet and ankle bones were strengthened, and leaping up, he stood! This is what we are to see! The text goes on to say he entered into the temple, walking, leaping, and praising God! Everyone knew it was him, and they all came running to Solomon's porch, filled with wonder and amazement at the spectacle (Acts 3:7–10).

When the disciples were in the Upper Room after Messiah was crucified and buried, for three days they had been praying the Amidah three times a day. A prayer they knew by heart from a four-hundred-year-old tradition was at the core of their beliefs. Here is another prayer/blessing they were praying from the Amidah:

> You, O Lord, are mighty forever, you revive the dead, you have the power to save. You sustain the living with loving-kindness, you revive the dead with great mercy, you support the falling, heal the sick, set free the bound and keep faith with those who sleep in the dust. Who is like you, O doer of mighty acts? Who resembles you, a king who puts to death and restores to life, and causes salvation to flourish? And you are certain to revive the dead. Blessed are you, O Lord, who revives the dead!

Can you believe this? Imagine the disciples praying this prayer three times a day every day after Yeshua had been buried. They were trying to put all their faith into their prayers. What's really crazy is the phrase that says God causes "salvation to flourish." The Hebrew word for "flourish" could also be translated as "resurrect," which is the theme of this prayer. The Hebrew word for "salvation" is *Yeshua*! So, they were actually praying, "Who resembles You, a King who puts to death and restores to life and causes *Yeshua to resurrect*!" Isn't this absolutely incredible?

Let's walk through Resurrection Sunday's events, it being the first day of the week. Now, remember: the "first day" of creation went from evening to morning (Gen. 1:5). So the first day of the week actually begins Saturday night and goes through sunset on Sunday night. We don't know exactly what time Messiah rose, but we do know the tomb was empty in the morning. He could have risen anytime Saturday night after sunset, since that begins the first day of the week.

In the morning, while it was still dark, Mary Magdalene saw the stone was rolled away and ran to tell Peter and John. They also checked it out, but the Bible tells us that they still didn't realize that the Scriptures said, "He must rise again," so they went home (John 20:1–10). Then Yeshua appeared before Mary, and she thought He was the gardener—until He revealed Himself to her. Again she raced to tell the disciples (vv. 14–18). Luke 24:10 says, "It was Mary Magdalene and Joanna, and Mary the mother of James, and other women that were with them, which told these things to the apostles."

That evening, all the disciples were assembled together, wondering if the story was true. Luke 24:11 says the women's words "seemed to them as idle tales" and they didn't believe. Earlier that afternoon, the two who were on the road to Emmaus had turned around and raced back to Jerusalem to confirm what the women had said earlier, after Yeshua appeared to them. But Mark 16:13 says no one believed them either!

You know how, when we pray the Scriptures often, we believe for a miracle and then—bam!—it happens? Here they were, fervently praying that what the others had said about Yeshua was true, when all of sudden, He appeared!

So here is the question. Is the Lord the same yesterday, today, and forever? Do you really believe that, or is it just a pet saying? If you really believe that statement is true in the depth of your being, then you will come to the same conclusion I did. If the Lord truly stays the same, then if He fulfilled the spring feasts to the day of His first coming, He will fulfill the fall feasts to the day of His second coming! Wrap your prophetic mind around that.

I am by no means setting dates. I am merely saying that the prophetic divine appointments that Israel had been rehearsing will be fulfilled again on those very days some year in the future. Therefore, we need to have an understanding prophetically of what is supposed to happen during the days of the fall feasts, because some year they will happen on the days appointed.

This is why the book of Revelation doesn't mention barley or wheat, because just as Christ's first coming was fulfilled in the spring feasts, the prophetic fulfillments of His second coming will happen in the fall. Instead, we read about a grape harvest, because this is the timing of the fall feasts (Rev. 14:18–20)!

Many believers feel they are to be in the dark concerning the coming of the Messiah. They are proud of their ignorance about the end-time and are determined to remain in darkness. When the Bible talks about knowing the times and seasons, you should realize by now that it is referring to the biblical calendar, not to winter or summer! Look at what the Bible says in 1 Thessalonians and meditate on it for a while:

> But concerning the times and the seasons, brethren, you have no need that I should write to you. For you yourselves know perfectly that the day of the Lord so comes as a thief in the night. For when they say, "Peace and safety!" then sudden destruction comes upon them, as labor pains upon a pregnant woman. And they shall not escape. But you, brethren, are not in darkness, so that this Day should overtake you as a thief. You are all sons of light and sons of the day. We are not of the night nor of darkness. (5:1–5 NKJV)

Yes, the Lord will come as a thief in the night. But when you read in context *who* that Day will "overtake as a thief," you can see that it is the dead church, the sleeping church, or in Yeshua's parables, the foolish virgins and the evil servants (Matt. 25:1–13; 24:45–51).

Don't have the Lord come to *you* as a thief in the night. Get on His calendar; come to the dress rehearsals, and discover some of the most exciting truths possible within His Word!

4

ANSWERING OBJECTIONS

I hope you have made the connections by now that enable you to see how important it is to be on God's calendar. Now I want to take some time to answer some common objections people have to abiding by God's calendar, so you will be rock solid in your understanding of its importance.

Many people misinterpret Bible verses and concepts by not looking at them in context. One of the passages often misunderstood is Galatians 4:8–11, where Paul told the Galatians that when they were pagans and didn't know God at all, they worshipped those who by nature were not gods. He went on to reprimand them, saying that now that they *do* know the true God, why in the world would they want to go back and be in bondage again to the "weak and beggarly elements"? He specifically mentioned their desire to return to their pagan calendar in observing days, months, times, and years.

Some readers believe he was talking about the biblical calendar in this passage. That is ridiculous. The Galatians were never on the biblical calendar, so how could they return to it? Pay close attention to the terms he used as well, such as *days* and *months*, which prove he was not talking about God's calendar at all. Whenever he referred to the biblical calendar, as in Colossians 2:16, he used the terms *holy day*, *Sabbath day*, *new moon*, and so forth. So what actually was going on here in Galatians?

To understand, you have to go to the beginning of the Galatians story, which is actually in the book of Acts. The Galatians and Ephesians were neighbors. In Acts 19 we read about the riot that took place in Ephesus when the townspeople were worshipping the great goddess Diana and the image they believed had fallen down from Jupiter. In Acts 14 we read about the Galatians who wanted to worship Paul and Barnabas, calling them Mercury and Jupiter and thinking the gods had come down in the likeness of men (v. 12 wyc). Paul cried out telling them to turn from these vanities to the living God, who'd made the heavens, earth, sea, and everything within. We see from this encounter that the Galatians worshipped the planets. The calendar they followed was much like the ones used for horoscopes today or perhaps the Chinese calendar, with the year of the pig, and so on. So now we realize that in Galatians 4 he was really asking, "Why are you returning to your *pagan* calendar, following horoscopes, and worshipping the planets again? You now have *God's* calendar of *divine* appointments, so why would you want to observe pagan holidays again?" There is no way a Jewish rabbi would refer to God's divine appointments "as weak and beggarly elements"! Common sense tells you that if Paul were recommending they turn back to the God of Israel, then he would not simultaneously tell them to disregard what the God of Israel had decreed or that His calendar is inadequate.

This gives us a better understanding of the other often-misinterpreted verse from Colossians. The Colossians did not want their neighbors the Galatians to return to the pagan calendar; they knew the importance of God's calendar. We know this from the terms Paul used. In verse 16 he told them to not let others (like the Galatians) judge them for keeping the holy days, Sabbath days, and new moons, which are a "shadow of things to come." This phrase further elevates their status. A "shadow" is proof positive of the reality of a thing, and here the verse is referring to things *to come*, not things from the past. I *want* an idea of what is coming. The feast days are the shadow, or patterns, of what not only came before, but is yet to come!

Now, some religious people say I'm preaching legalism. That's absurd. I am not saying you have to follow God's calendar to be saved. We are saved only by grace through faith, and not by our works (Eph. 2:8–9). But we are saved that we might *do* the works of God (v. 10)! And because we are saved, we should do what God asks. And here is where you need to understand the working of the devil.

We live in the age of lawlessness. The spirit of the Antichrist, satan's "man of sin," is already at work (2 Thess. 2:7–10). Satan does not want you on God's calendar. He wants you to miss the divine appointments. So his ministers appear as ministers of light, to deceive you (2 Cor. 11:14–15). And many *will* be deceived because of their hyper-grace teachings. According to them, you may sin all you want without fear because of God's "grace." Anyone who teaches obedience to what God says is branded a legalist. I've seen, heard, and read about religious leaders who claim to be righteous but are totally opposed to God's laws. Whenever I mention following God's laws, an antichrist spirit rises up within them and they almost start foaming at the mouth, saying, "Don't put *me* under God's law! I'm not *under* the law!" You can feel the hatred. Their argument is always "Jesus fulfilled that!" Well, wait a minute. "Are you saying we don't have to love one another because 'Jesus fulfilled that,'?" I ask them. "Or are you saying I can now steal or murder or commit adultery because 'Jesus fulfilled that'?" They may complain that that is not what they are saying, but what they are saying is practically the same thing. If we know that God desires it, we should do it. Just because I say we should follow God's laws and obey Him rather than man does not mean I am saying we are saved through the law or that I am advocating legalism.

Let me give you an example of a real legalist. Leviticus 19:9 tells farmers not to reap the corners of their fields but to leave them for the poor and strangers. A legalist would say that since he is not a farmer, he never has to give to the poor or to strangers. A child of God would say that even though he is not a farmer he understands God's heart, so regardless he will give to the poor and to strangers. Here is another example. Also in Leviticus 19:13 God basically says that employers should pay their employees on time. How would you like your employer to tell you that he is "not under the law" so he doesn't "have to pay you on payday!" Jesus fulfilled that! Do you see the absurdity in this? In no way do I believe we are saved by keeping the Law, which is how many define legalism.

Am I trying to make everyone Jewish? No! I am simply exhorting people to do what God says.

There is a very strong anti-Semitic spirit within the church today that is truly demonic. Your spirit will witness this when you hear religious leaders and others who are so vocally opposed to anything that even smells Jewish. I don't know what they will do when they find out Yeshua is Jewish, with Jewish parents! There's a reason He is known as the King of the Jews.

When I got saved forty years ago and went to Bible college, we studied the feasts of the Lord. Sure, we saw the typology of Christ in them, but for heaven's sake, we would never celebrate them! "They're Jewish, and that would be legalistic!" was the thinking. I learned the absurdity of that mind-set over twenty years ago when I actually started celebrating them.

You don't learn how to build a building by simply studying architecture in college. You really understand when you actually *build* a building. It's the same with God's Word. Too many people pat themselves on the back for studying God's Word, but they never do it! In the next chapter, we will look at practical ways to apply God's Word with respect to His calendar.

5

PRACTICAL APPLICATION

How do we keep Passover today? First, remember what Yeshua said: "Do this in memory of me" (Luke 22:19 CJB). So for believers, we at El Shaddai Ministries believe "do this" means "do this," so we celebrate Passover as a remembrance of what Yeshua did two thousand years ago. No, we don't sacrifice any lambs! But every year, we do have a Passover Seder as a memorial of what Yeshua did. We probably have one of the world's largest Passover events, bringing meaning to what the Messiah did on the cross. We have had over fifteen hundred people attend our event. All of them were non-Jews who marvel at how Yeshua fulfilled the Passover in so much detail. Thousands more watched the live stream service, and over two hundred thousand have watched the archives we have on our website for free. All our feast services are archived so any congregation or family can watch, to come up with ideas on how to celebrate them on their own. In this chapter, as well as in appendix 1, I will give you the "bones" of a Seder service and show you how we at El Shaddai Ministries put flesh on it based on our belief in the Messiah.

The Passover Seder has its foundation in Exodus, where the four stages of redemption are found. God said He had heard the groanings of the children of Israel, whom the Egyptians had enslaved, and that He remembered His covenant. Notice all the "I will" actions that God said He would take (Ex. 6:6–7):

1. "I will bring you out from under the burdens of the Egyptians."

2. "I will rid you out of their bondage."

3. "I will redeem you with a stretched out arm, and with great judgments."

4. "I will take you to me for a people, and I will be to you a God."

These are known as the *four cups of salvation*. The first cup, where He promised to bring us out from under our burdens, is known as the *cup of sanctification*. God picked Israel and set them apart from the nations to redeem. Recognize that if God removed the heavy burdens they were carrying, He also wants to remove your load!

The second cup is known as the *cup of deliverance*. It is great when God removes our burdens, but the problem for Israel was that they were still chained to Egypt! So there are different phases to our total redemption. God sanctifies and sets us apart with the first cup, removing our burdens. Then He delivers us by breaking the chains that keep us in bondage with the second cup. How many of us, even after we are saved, still have habits that are hard to break? During the Seder we drink from four cups, asking God to complete each stage of the redemption process for us.

The third cup, where He says, "I will redeem you with a stretched out arm," is known as the *cup of redemption*. It is also known as the cup after supper. Jews drink from the first two cups before the meal, and the other two cups after the meal. We see this even in Yeshua's time in the book of Luke, where at the Last Seder Yeshua took the cup, gave thanks, and said, "Take this, and divide it among yourselves" (22:17). Then He took the bread, representing His body, and told the disciples to break the bread in remembrance of Him. Finally, he took the "cup after supper," telling them that this cup was the cup of the new covenant in His blood, which would be shed for them (v. 20). So the third cup, the cup of redemption, is taken after the meal. Judas left before the taking of the third cup. Symbolically, this cup is what pays the price for our redemption. This is so needed because though the first cup relieves us of our burdens, and the second cup delivers from our bondage, we still have a problem! We are still in Egypt! A redemption price has to be paid, just as when you redeem something from a pawn shop. We have been bought with a price. While our redemption was free to us, it came at great expense!

What totally blows my mind about this cup is that God said He would redeem us with an outstretched *arm*. Not a hand, but an arm. If you threw a baseball with just your hand, it wouldn't go nearly as far as it would if you included the power of your full arm. It took an extension of God's power to redeem you. With this in mind, go to the book of Jeremiah and read how God made the earth, man, and beast as well by His great power and "outstretched arm" (27:4–5). This tells us it took the same extension of God's power to redeem us as it did for creation!

By the way, what did it cost God to create the earth? Absolutely nothing. He just spoke it into being. As a matter of fact, if it all disappeared today, God could re-create it with just a word. If we were to try to calculate the financial worth of the entire world based on its land; its resources, such as gold, silver, platinum, trees, and water; and add in the price of all the real estate in the entire world, it would be astronomical! Yet God sees little value in it, as it really didn't cost Him a thing.

But look at the cost to God in redeeming you. It cost Him everything. Specifically, it cost Him the life of His Son! This shows you how much more valuable you are to God than all the resources in the entire world combined! This is why we must love people and use things, not love things and use people!

The Hebrew word for redemption is *goel*. It is made up of one of the names of God: El (אל) with the letter *gimel* (ג) in front of it: גאל. The letter *gimel* means to "lift up." This teaches us that redemption comes when God is lifted up!

This brings us to the fourth and much-needed cup: the *cup of acceptance*. It would have been enough if He just removed our burdens. It would have been more than enough that He also delivered us from our bondage, and then paid the price to redeem us. But now He even wants to marry us? That's what He meant when He said, "I will bring you to me for a people." Isn't it incredible to know we have been accepted in the beloved (Eph. 1:6)?

See, God could have taken Israel's burdens, delivered them from bondage, paid the price to redeem them, brought them out of Egypt—then just dumped them out in the desert, saying, "Here you go; see you later!" After all, just because you are nice and bail someone out of jail, it doesn't mean you also want to marry her! But instead, God told Israel that He wanted to enter into a *relationship* with her.

There is also a fifth cup actually, known as the cup of Elijah.

This cup is placed at an empty seat set aside for Elijah, as it is believed that some year on Passover, Elijah will show up and declare that the messianic kingdom has arrived. This is based on Malachi 4, where the Lord says, "I will send you Elijah the prophet before the coming of the great and dreadful day of the LORD," in order to "turn the hearts of the fathers to the children, and the hearts of the children to the fathers" (vv. 5–6). This is from our text in Exodus 6 after the fourth cup, where it now adds:

5. "I will bring you to the land that I swore to give to Abraham, Isaac, and Jacob, and I will give it to you for a possession" (v. 8 HCSB).

Abraham, Isaac, and Jacob are the early church "fathers"— the very ones meant in Malachi.

There are also the stories of the four sons that are a part of every Passover Seder. These come from the Scriptures and reveal four different attitudes children—and for that matter, adults—display concerning the Seder. We'll begin with the innocent son, who doesn't yet know he should even question the meaning of the Seder. The Bible says you are to tell this son, "This is done because of what the LORD did for me when I came up from Egypt" (Ex. 13:8 NKJV). Based on this text, it is taught that each of us should see ourselves as coming out of Egypt.

The next son is known as the simple son, who is all excited about the Passover Seder and initiates the conversation, but really has no understanding. Exodus 13:14 tells parents how to answer this son.

Then there is the wise son, who has a great vocabulary: "What is the meaning of the testimonies, the statutes, and the judgments which the LORD our God has commanded you?" he asks (Deut. 6:20 NKJV). You are to respond that we observe them to "fear the Lord" and because they are only for our good so that we might be preserved alive. In doing this it will be accounted to us as righteousness (vv. 24–25).

Finally, there is the rebellious son, who asks, "What do you mean by this *service?*" (Ex. 12:26 NKJV; emphasis added). The Hebrew word used here for "service" implies bondage or slave labor. So this son considers the Seder to be nothing but a burden. In modern days it would be compared to "Don't you put *me* under the law!" I love the answer given to this child. It's like, "Look kid: this is the sacrifice of the *Lord's* Passover. When He passed over the houses of the people in Egypt, He *struck* the Egyptians, but spared our houses." It's almost as if to say, "So you better shape up!"

Another aspect of the Seder you may want to implement is reclining when you drink from the four cups and eat the matzah. In ancient times only free people had the luxury of reclining while eating; slaves had to stand. In the Seder, traditionally everyone leans to the left. This is significant because on either side of the father or leader of the Seder was a seat, each assigned to a particular person. The youngest child would be seated on the right; the oldest, on the left. At Yeshua's last Seder, the apostle John was the youngest person present, which is why he was to the right of Yeshua, leaning upon Him. So, who was the oldest? It was Judas the betrayer! Judas sat to Yeshua's left, which is why after He dipped the matzah, He simply turned and gave it to him. So Yeshua would have been leaning on Judas!

* * *

Now that we have studied Passover and talked about how we celebrate it at El Shaddai Ministries, you are ready to practice it for yourself. At the back of the book, I have provided the steps for a simple Seder for believers, so that you and your family or church community can celebrate Passover together. It will only increase your love for the Lord and will make you more aware of His great love and sacrifice for you.

Now we will turn our attention to the first of the fall feasts: Rosh Hashanah.

6

ROSH HASHANAH

Realizing that the spring feasts of the Bible were actually fulfilled in the spring, to the very day on God's divine day timer, the question to which we now turn is what, prophetically, will happen on the fall feast days? From the biblical pattern we have seen, we now know that the fulfillment of each feast will take place in the fall, on the day of the feast. Each year, when Israel kept each of the fall feasts, they were going through a dress rehearsal of what would happen on that very day, some year in the future.

Remember: we are not setting dates, as we have no idea what year the events will unfold. But we can have a prophetic understanding of what may happen some year on these divine appointments as we study what was being rehearsed.

Before we continue, it is important to know two key points. First, the fall feasts are sequential in their fulfillments. For example, the Ruach HaKodesh, or Holy Spirit, could not have been poured out until Messiah had ascended to heaven. Yeshua could not have ascended to heaven until He rose from the dead. He couldn't rise from the dead until He was buried, and He couldn't be buried before He'd died! The same will be true with the fulfillments of the Fall Feasts. Rosh Hashanah must be prophetically realized first, then Yom Kippur, followed by the Feast of Tabernacles, which we'll study momentarily.

The second point is that each feast day may have multiple fulfillments. For example, Rosh Hashanah, also known as the Feast of Trumpets, may be fulfilled several times over a period of years. We read about seven trumpets sounding in the book of Revelation. Well, these trumpets could be spread out over the seven years of the Tribulation, with one blast happening each year on the Feast of Trumpets.

The problem with our thinking is that we are often victims of the Greek mind-set, which sees "fulfilling" something as checking it off of a checklist. *Okay, we're done with that now. Moving on . . .* But in the Bible, fulfillment is more like, *This has happened before, so you can sure believe it will happen again!*

So let's unpack the truths behind the first of our fall feasts: Rosh Hashanah. To begin with, it has several names, each revealing different aspects. Just as I can be a father, a brother, an uncle, a nephew, and a grandpa all at the same time, Rosh Hashanah, which means the "Head of the Year," is several *different* things, all in one. First, it is known as the head of the year because it marks the first day of the civil calendar as far as the biblical calendar goes. Much like January 1 on the world's calendar, Rosh Hashanah, then, is the Jewish New Year. This is the day when Adam opened his eyes for the very first time and crowned God as King.

Biblically, Rosh Hashanah is known as "Yom Teruah," meaning the "Day of Blowing." This comes from Numbers 29:1. God told us that we are to observe it on the first day of the seventh month of the religious calendar, known as Tishri, which is the first month of the civil calendar. Yom Teruah is a day for blowing the shofar.

Teruah, which means "blowing," also means "to shout," as in a battle cry. Psalm 47:5 speaks of God going up with a "shout" and the sound of the "trumpet," or shofar. This is referring directly to the pre-appointed day when God Himself will shout the battle cry as He comes to judge the earth, and will blow the shofar to gather His troops! This is what the apostle Paul was referring to when he wrote in 1 Thessalonians 4:16 that "the Lord himself will descend from heaven with a shout . . . and with the blast of God's shofar. The dead in Messiah will rise first" (HNV). Do you realize this is the very day of the resurrection of the dead? The so-called rapture, then, is not an "any moment" event, because the resurrection of the dead is a *scheduled* event! We have no idea what year it will occur, but Yom Teruah is the day of the dress rehearsal for it! Just as Adam rose from the dust on this day and crowned God as King of the universe, man will again rise from the dust of the earth on the same day and crown Him Lord of all. This has been taught for several thousand years. We find it in the Jewish writings or commentaries from the Talmud in Rosh Hashanah 16b.

Daniel 12:1 tells us that at that time Michael, the angel of Israel, will stand up, and "there shall be a time of trouble, such as never was since there was a nation even to that same time" (HNV). One of the other names for Rosh Hashanah is "the Time of Trouble"! The verse goes on to say, "At that time your people shall be delivered, everyone who shall be found written in the book" (HNV). Incredibly, another name for Rosh Hashanah is "the Opening of the Books"!

Daniel continues by saying that many of those who sleep in the dust of the earth shall awake, some to everlasting life, and some to shame and everlasting contempt. Guess what: Rosh Hashanah is also known as "the Day of the Awakening Blast"! This is why Psalm 89:15 says the people who know the joyful shout are blessed and will be the ones to walk in the light of God's face!

In 1 Corinthians 15:52, the apostle Paul said that we shall all be changed in the "twinkling of an eye." Did you know this also was the phrase used by the sages to refer to the day of redemption? Paul went on to say that this will happen at the "last trump," for the shofar shall sound and the dead will rise. My goodness! Do you realize that when he wrote about the resurrection happening at the "last trump," he was referring to the last blast of the shofar on the Feast of Trumpets? On this day the shofar is blown one hundred times. The hundreth blast is known as the "Last Trump"!

There are three sounds made by the shofar on the Feast of Trumpets.[1] First there is the *Tekiah*, which is a single long blast. Then there is the *Shevarim*, which consists of three short blasts. There is also the *Teruah*, consisting of nine short blasts in quick succession. The word *Teruah* can also refer to the sounding of an "alarm," as in Numbers 10, where God says that when the enemy comes at you, if you blow an alarm with the shofar, He will remember you and save you (v. 9). Finally, the last blast is a special blast, known as the *Tekiah Gedolah*. In English that means the "Great Big Blast"!

Yom Teruah is also known as the "day of remembrance." So if you remember to crown God as King and sound the shofar on the Feast of Trumpets, God will remember you and save you from your enemies! Yom Teruah is the sounding of the alarm clock to tell the dead it is time to wake up!

This theme is also found in the Song of Songs, a beautiful poetic book about a bridegroom and his bride. The bride continually falls asleep, and the bridegroom's voice is what wakes her up. In the Bible, death is often referred to as sleep.

In the second chapter, the bride didn't just have a long night's sleep; she went into hibernation! In verses 10 and 11, she hears the bridegroom's voice waking her up with the words "The winter is past, the rain is over and gone"! In chapter 5 she is asleep again, but says her heart awoke at the sound of her beloved's voice (vv. 2–6).[2] In verse 2 the Hebrew word for sleep is the same word used for those who "sleep" in the dust of the earth. We read that she hears his voice knocking. The Hebrew word for "knocks" there does not mean to lightly rap, but to beat soundly, as if he is pounding on the door. It's almost as if she is at the point of death, but her heart begins to beat as he is pounding on her chest as if doing CPR to bring her back to life. The bridegroom goes on to proclaim that his head is filled with dew and his locks with the drops of the night. In the Bible dew is tied to the resurrection of the dead. We see this in Isaiah 26:19, which states, "Your dead men shall live, together with my dead body shall they arise." This verse goes on to tell those who dwell in the dust to "awake and sing" for "the earth shall cast out the dead." This is why the Feast of Trumpets is known as the Day of the Awakening Blast!

I just get so excited about keeping these festivals. God loves to throw a party, and He invites His kids to come. I don't know if your heart is racing as fast as I am typing this, but I just feel like a kid in a candy store as I see God's hand all over this! You know how sometimes people outrun themselves and trip because they are going too fast? That's how I get when

I am writing, and have to slow down and regroup, as I am having so much fun!

When you understand these concepts, you realize Rabbi Paul was referring to the Feast of Trumpets when he warned the Ephesians to wake up and arise from the dead (Eph. 5:14). The thundering of God's voice is what will wake the dead. This is why the term the "voice of the Lord" is associated with the Feast of Trumpets, as His voice comes as the sound of the shofar! We see this at Mount Sinai when He comes down in Exodus 19, as well as in Revelation 1:10, where John hears God's voice as a shofar. Psalm 29 is also read every Feast of Trumpets, and you will see why. It repeatedly refers to the voice of the LORD. Verse 3 speaks of the voice of the Lord thundering on the waters. Verse 4 says the voice of the Lord is powerful and full of majesty. Verse 5 says His voice "breaks the cedars." In verses 7 and 8 the voice of the Lord divides the flames of fire and shakes the wilderness. In verse 9 it makes the hinds to calve. It concludes with verses 10 and 11, where God is sitting on His throne as King forever and blessing His people with peace.

And finally, Rosh Hashanah is the day of the coronation of the Messiah! Don't you want to be there for the coronation? I know I sure do! How religious people can call the dress rehearsal for the coronation of Messiah "legalism" is beyond me! If they want to be dried-up prunes, with scowl on their faces because of their anti-Semitism and Pharisaic attitude, so be it! They won't stop *me* from going to the dress rehearsal for the coronation of the King of kings and Lord of lords! Don't let them keep you from the party either!

You know how at sporting events, the crowd sometimes does the "wave"? One year I thought it would be great to have a wave of the blowing of shofars in every time zone around the world, so people from every nation could proclaim God as King as the Feast of Trumpets arrived in their individual time zones. Then everyone around the world would blow his or her shofar when it was time for Jerusalem to celebrate. It was such a success that we do it every year now! People come to our website and sign up so we can be sure every time zone is covered. Can you imagine how this blesses the heart of God? People of every language remembering Him on the day He appointed as the "day of remembrance"!

When I finally realized one of the keys to unlocking prophecy was understanding that these feast days were dress rehearsals for the days the events will happen, it literally rocked my world. Do you realize just how big the event will be when Messiah comes? Do you believe God preplanned this event? I believe it is so big that every year they go through the dress rehearsal in heaven! Imagine every year on Rosh Hashanah the angelic host is rehearsing the coming of the Messiah. At the same time here on earth, all those with understanding are simultaneously rehearsing the same event! It's like a harmonic resonance. We become one with what is going on in heaven at the very same time. Some year on that day, the dress rehearsal will become the reality, and we will simply instantaneously be translated to the party! It will all seem so natural, as we are already recognizing the appointed time! Do you want to be at the dress rehearsal? Then join the party with your friends and neighbors, or join ours by live streaming!

By the way, for those who say I am in this for the money, let me remind you that our teachings are free, the live stream is free, the audio is free, and the notes can be downloaded for *free*. Anyone interested can go to our web archives at elshaddaiministries.us and watch our previous feast services to see how to practically keep these important events for themselves.

I have to say, our congregation is weird! We have people from a multitude of nations who attend: Koreans, Russians, Central Americans, South Americans, Indians, Europeans, Native Americans, African Americans, you name it! We even do ASL. We also have folks from every denomination come. We have Catholics, Baptists, Pentecostals, Lutherans, Methodists, Presbyterians, and many more as we meet on the Shabbat so they can still attend their own services on Sunday. But I digress.

On Rosh Hashanah, the coronation of God as King is an oft-repeated theme during the morning prayers. It is even chanted by the cantor as he opens the morning prayers crowning God as the King of the universe. We see from the book of 2 Samuel that the kings of Israel were anointed, as when the elders anointed David king in Hebron (2 Sam. 5:3). Later we also see Solomon being anointed, followed by the blowing of the shofar (1 Kings 1:34–39). Genesis 49:10 tells us that the scepter will "not depart from Judah" until Shiloh come, which is a reference to the Messiah. It goes on to say that to Him will "the gathering of the people be."

Psalm 47 is known as the coronation psalm and is part of the Rosh Hashanah service every year. Can you imagine what that day will be like for the redeemed! It takes my breath away. As you read over some of the verses from Psalm 47 here, imagine you are there and hear the noise!

O clap your hands, all you people; shout to God with the voice of triumph. [Remember: *Teruah* means "to shout."]

For the LORD most high is . . . a great King over all the earth.

He shall subdue the people under us, and the nations under our feet. . . .

God is gone up with a shout, the LORD with the sound of a trumpet [shofar].

Sing praises to God, sing praises: sing praises to our King, sing praises.

For God is the King of all the earth: sing you praises with understanding.

God reigns over the heathen: God sits on the throne of his holiness.

The princes of the people are gathered together, even the people of the God of Abraham [to pledge their allegiance to God].

Remember how Romans 8:22 says that the whole creation is groaning in travail, waiting for redemption? Psalm 98 tells us that at the sound of the shofar, the Lord will be proclaimed King, and even the floods will clap their hands and the hills will be joyful as He comes to judge the earth (vv. 6, 8). Talk about a different sound!

But the shofar blast also comes as a warning to God's people. In Ezekiel, God told the prophet to hear His word and then blow the shofar to warn the people for Him (Ezek. 33:2–7). That is what this feast is all about. It is a day of warning. The problem in the prophets' day was the attitude of the people. God declared that their ears were uncircumcised, and they could not listen. He set watchman over them, telling them to heed the sound of the shofar, but they said they *would* not listen. God said to ask for the ancient paths, where the good way is, and they would find rest for their souls, but they said they didn't *want* to walk in the old paths (Jer. 6:10–19). Don't let this be your attitude! In Isaiah 58:1 God told the prophet to lift up his voice like a shofar and to show His people their transgressions. My desire is to sound the shofar, that God's people might repent and come to the feasts!

Another name for Rosh Hashanah is Yom HaDin, which means the Day of Judgment. Kingship and judgment are closely linked. Every year on this day, it is believed that the doors of the heavenly court are opened and court is in session. During the following ten days, to Yom Kippur, God determines who will live and who will die the next year. On Yom Kippur the doors close and judgment is then meted out. So God not only sits on His throne as King on Rosh Hashanah, but He also judges all mankind. Therefore, this day is also known as the opening of the gates, opening of the doors, and the opening of the books. Where do we see all this in Scripture? Let's take a look.

In 2 Corinthians 5:10 we read that everyone is to appear before the judgment seat of Messiah, that we may receive His ruling on what we have done in this life, whether good or bad. In his first letter to the Corinthians, Paul wrote that all of our works will be manifest, "for the day shall declare it." What "day" was he referring to? Rosh Hashanah! The passage goes on to say that if after going through the fire, all of one's works are burned up and he has nothing to show for it, he is still saved, as we are not saved by our works, but how sad for him that he had built his foundation with wood, hay, and stubble rather than gold, silver, and precious stones. The fiery stream from God's courthouse left him with nothing (1 Cor. 3:12–15).

We must remember that everything happening on earth was based on a pattern in heaven. Moses was told to build the tabernacle after this heavenly pattern (Num. 8:4; Ex. 25:9). Where else in Scripture do we see the concepts of Rosh Hashanah, with God sitting on His throne, judgment being meted out through fire, and books being opened?

In Daniel 7, the prophet beheld the coronation of the King and simultaneous judgment (vv. 9–11). A fiery stream issued from before Him, while a thousand thousands ministered to Him and ten thousand times ten thousand stood before Him. Then the judgment was set and the books were opened, and the beast who had defied God was slain and given over to the burning flame!

What's amazing to me is this is exactly what John saw in the book of Revelation! In chapter 5 John hears the "voice of many angels" around the throne, and "ten thousand times ten thousand, and thousands of thousands" declaring with a loud voice, "Worthy is the Lamb that was slain to receive power, and riches, and wisdom, and strength, and honor, and glory, and blessing" (vv. 11–13). Then every creature in heaven, on earth, and under the sea also responds in kind to Him that sits on the throne. In Revelation 20:11–12, John saw a great white throne. The dead were standing before God, and the books were opened. Then another book was opened and the dead were judged based on what was written in the books, according to their works.

We talk about Rosh Hashanah being the day of the opening of the doors, the sound of the shofar, the voice of the Lord, and a throne being set in heaven, and it makes me wonder what day John was seeing in Revelation 4? It says he saw a door opening in heaven! He heard a voice like a trumpet, or shofar, talking with him! The voice told him he would be shown what is coming, and immediately he was in the Spirit and beheld a throne in heaven, with Someone sitting on it (vv. 1–11)! Throughout the chapter, worship is given to the one seated on the throne, before whom the elders cast their crowns, declaring He is worthy to receive glory and honor and power! Was John seeing the future Rosh Hashanah, when these events will unfold? Hello! Of course he was! Rosh Hashanah is the opening of the gates, when the Lord comes in judgment! Listen to Psalm 24:

> Lift up your heads, O you gates; and be you lift up, you everlasting doors; and the King of glory shall come in. Who is this King of glory? The LORD strong and mighty, the LORD mighty in battle. Lift up your heads, O you gates; even lift them up, you everlasting doors; and the King of glory shall come in. Who is this King of glory? The LORD of hosts, he is the King of glory. (vv. 7–10)

Earlier we learned that Psalm 118 is read on the feast days. Check out verses 19 and 20:

> Open to me the gates of righteousness: I will go into them, and I will praise the LORD: This gate of the LORD, into which the righteous shall enter.

In the book of Matthew we read about when the Son of man comes in His glory and sits on His throne of glory. It says that He will gather the nations and separate them as sheep from goats based on how they treated the nation of Israel (25:31–46). Compare this to Isaiah 26:2, where Judah sings, "Open you the gates, that the righteous nation which keeps the truth may enter in."

Rosh Hashanah is also known as the "Hidden Day." If you continue reading in Isaiah 26, you will see that God's people are told to enter into their chambers, shut their doors, and "hide" themselves for a moment until the indignation is over, because the Lord is coming to punish the world for their iniquity (vv. 20–21). In Psalm 27:5 David wrote, "In the time of trouble [God] shall hide me in his pavilion; in the secret of his tabernacle shall he hide me." And Zephaniah 2 warns the meek of the earth to seek the Lord, so they may be hid in the day of His anger (vv. 1–4). I don't know about you but I'm all for being hid in the day of the Lord's anger!

Some say, "But I thought we aren't supposed to know the day or the hour, because Messiah will come as a thief in the night." First off, it is impossible to know the day or the hour anyway, because there are twenty-four time zones and it can be two different days at any one time. Plus, I do not claim to know the date, and I never have claimed to know it. We are to know the times and seasons, and as we have found out, the times and seasons specifically is referring to the appointed times! Paul told the Thessalonians, "Of the times and the seasons, brothers, you have no need that I write to you." Why? Because they already knew the appointed times! He went on to say that they know Messiah will come as a thief in the night. But then read very slowly what he said next: "But you, brothers, are not in darkness, that that day should overtake you as a thief" (1 Thess. 5:1–2, 4).

Remember: Messiah was upset at the religious leaders of His day because they could not discern the signs of the times (Matt. 16:3). Yeshua wept over Jerusalem because they didn't recognize the time of their visitation (Luke 19:41–44). We always need to look at the Bible in context. To whom does the Bible say the

Messiah will come as a thief in the night?

In the book of Revelation it is to the dead church of Sardis that He says He will come as a thief in the night because they are not watching (Rev. 3:1–3). If you are taught to not watch because Messiah will come as a thief, you might check the pulse of your church! We also find in Revelation the lukewarm, wretched, miserable, poor, blind, and naked church of Laodicea. They are told to put on white raiment that the shame of their nakedness doesn't show, and then they are to anoint their eyes that they might see. The problem that church had was they were lukewarm and prosperous not realizing they were really blind and naked (Rev. 3:17–18). We read again later in the book that Messiah will come as a thief in the night (16:15). It says further that those who are watching will be blessed because they keep their garments on. Those who do not watch are at risk of walking "naked," and people will see the shame of their nakedness. That sounds like the warning to the church of Laodicea. So, based on these passages the Messiah will come as a thief in the night to the dead church and to the lukewarm, prosperity-loving church that is really blind, wretched, poor, naked, and miserable!

Who else, in context, is not aware of the "day or the hour" of Christ's return? You have to realize this is a metaphor, and is not speaking of the literal day and hour, as no one can know that. It refers to the concept of not being able to understand the times and seasons of the feasts of the Lord. In the Gospel of Matthew, Yeshua tells a parable about some wise and foolish virgins. The wise are ready to go to the wedding, but the foolish are not. By the time they are ready, it is too late! It is to the foolish virgins, not the wise, that the Lord says, "I don't know you" (Matt. 25:8–13). To say you do not know someone is the same thing as saying I don't remember you! Remember! The Feast of Trumpets is the day of remembrance, and the foolish didn't remember but the wise did, so the Lord remembered them!

In Malachi we read about those who feared the Lord and spoke often to one another and the Lord heard them! Then it says there was set before the Lord a book of remembrance wherein was written the names of those who thought upon His name (Mal. 3:16–18). The Lord says that in the day when He makes up His jewels, those who feared Him will be spared, and then it will be known who the righteous and wicked are. People will be able to discern between those who truly serve God and those who don't.

In Messiah's parable about good and evil servants (Luke 12:37–46), the evil servants saw that the time of their lord's coming was delayed and began to mistreat their inferiors. It was to those evil servants who were not watching that their master came as a thief.

Two people cannot walk together unless they are agreed (Amos 3:3). So if you want to walk hand in hand with the Creator, know what's on His day timer, and be available.

The day of the Lord is also known as the "time of Jacob's trouble." In Jeremiah 30, the prophet asks, "Why do I see every man with his hands on his loins, as a woman in travail?" Jeremiah goes on to say, "Alas! for that day is great . . . none is like it: it is even the time of Jacob's trouble." Isaiah saw the same thing. "The day of the LORD is at hand!" he wrote, warning that every man's heart will melt on that day. Everyone will be afraid as pangs and sorrows "take hold of them." They will be just like a pregnant woman who is nearing the time of her delivery (Isa. 13:6–8; 26:17).

In Matthew we learn that before Christ's coming, nation will rise against nation A better translation would be ethnic group will rise against ethnic group. The passage goes on to say that there will be famines, pestilences, and earthquakes in various places—and that these are the beginning of sorrows (Matt. 24:7–8). The Greek definition for the word "sorrows" refers to labor pangs. We see the day of Yom Teruah and the blowing of shofars tied to the day of the Lord in the book of Zephaniah as well (Zeph. 1:14–16). There we are told that the great day of the Lord is near and is coming very quickly. It will be a day of wrath, of trouble and distress, of desolation, gloominess, clouds, and thick darkness. Then look at the very next association: Zephaniah called it a day of the trumpet, or shofar, and alarm. The Hebrew word for alarm here is *Teruah*!

Joel also ties the day of the Lord with the very day of Yom Teruah. Chapter 2 begins with the command to blow the trumpet and to sound an alarm, for the day of the Lord, a day of darkness and gloominess, comes (Joel 2:1–2).

Here comes another amazing connection. We will connect some dots as you connected numbers in grade school until it revealed a picture. The verses I will connect for you will reveal something that will totally surprise you.

Did you ever consider the book of Proverbs to contain end-time prophecy? Well, get a load of this! In Revelation 17:5 we see the name "Mystery, Babylon, the Mother of Harlots and Abominations of the Earth." In Daniel we learn that there will be an evil end-time king who will corrupt by flattery those who do wickedly against the covenant and will magnify himself above all (Dan. 11:32–38). Now go to Proverbs 7 and you will discover a prophecy there.

Proverbs 7:5 warns the reader about "the strange woman" who flatters with her words" (v. 5). Yet directly, a simple one, void of understanding, heads right to her house. Notice it is in the "black and dark night" and that the woman wears the attire of a harlot (vv. 7–10). In verse 14 we see she is a religious harlot. "I have peace offerings with me," she brags. Then she goes on to say that they should just take their fill of love until morning because the *master is not home*; he's "gone on a long journey." Compare this to Yeshua's story in Matthew 25, where the master, who represents Christ Himself, is "traveling to a far country" (v. 14).

So what does the harlot say at last? "The master . . . will come home at the day appointed" (Prov. 7:19–20)! Did you get that? Even the harlot knows there is a day *appointed* for Yeshua's return!

The Feast of Unleavened Bread and the Feast of Tabernacles are both at the full moon in the middle of the month. They were easy to determine by simply counting from the first to the fifteenth. But since the beginning of the months was determined by the sighting of the new moon, no one knew the day or the hour each month would begin. Because the Jews had been scattered throughout other countries, they would light fires on hillsides to pass the news along that the new moon had been sighted and confirmed by two witnesses, and that the first of the month had arrived. The Feast of Trumpets was to be celebrated on the first day of the month of Tishri. Because each day actually starts at sunset, and not in the morning, the first day would be half over when you woke up! So the Feast of Trumpets was celebrated for two days and was known as one long day. This was the one feast when no one would know the day or the hour that it would begin! This day was symbolically even hidden from satan; he wouldn't even be sure of its arrival.

Some prophecies are to remain secret and hidden until the appropriate time for their revelation. This is why the apostle John had to seal up and not write what the seven thunders uttered in Revelation 10. Daniel was also told to "shut up the words" of the prophecy he had been shown and "seal the book" until the "time of the end" (Dan. 12:4). The angel goes on to say that many will be purified, and made white, but the wicked shall do wickedly, and none of them will understand; only the wise will (v. 10). When that same chapter says that in the end-time, knowledge will be increased (v. 4), I believe this can mean an increased understanding of the Bible as God begins to reveal secrets. Deuteronomy 29:29 says that the secret things belong to the Lord, but those things that are revealed belong to those who will do the words of the Torah.

Another name for the Feast of Trumpets is HaKiddushin/Nisu'in or the Wedding of the Messiah. We read in Isaiah that as a young man marries a virgin and as the bridegroom rejoices over the bride, so shall God rejoice over you (Isa. 62:5). The "you" there is Jerusalem, as the chapter goes on to say that those who make mention of the Lord are not to keep silent but are to give God no rest until He makes Jerusalem a praise in the earth (vv. 6–7). Jerusalem is seen as the bride in Revelation 21:2 as well.

So why is this particular day considered a wedding day? Because it takes us back to creation, where we have the first wedding, between Adam and Eve, on this day! God Himself was the Officiate, and heaven and earth were the two witnesses. In a Jewish wedding there are seven blessings said over the bride and groom. Almost all of them take us back to creation. Within the seven blessings are blessings to the Creator for the creation of the fruit of the vine, the One who created everything for

His glory, the Creator of human beings, who also gladdened His creatures in the garden of Eden. Then there is a blessing to God, as the King of the universe, who created joy and gladness, the groom and bride, mirth, glad song, pleasure, delight, love, brotherhood, peace, and companionship. By mentioning creation, the blessing alludes to a future time also, when God's purposes for mankind will be consummated.

In the book of Joel, where we earlier read about the day of the Lord, we see a command to blow the trumpet in Zion, to gather the people, and to sanctify them (Joel 2:15–16). Notice that it talks of the bridegroom leaving his chamber and the bride coming out of her closet. The Hebrew word for closet here is *chuppah*, the traditional wedding canopy under which Jewish couples are married.

The concept of Yom Teruah and a wedding go hand in hand. There are two parts to the coming together of the couple. The first is called the *kiddushin*, which is the rite of betrothal. This is where the groom asks the woman for her hand in marriage; if she accepts, they are betrothed to each other. She is sanctified, or set apart, for only him until the time of the second part, the *nisu'in*, or the actual wedding day, in which the rite is completed. Traditionally the bride and groom refrain from seeing each other for a full week before the wedding to increase their yearning for each other.

Typically, marriages were arranged by the parents, as was the case with Abraham in finding a bride for his son Isaac. The young man would go to the house of the bride carrying three items: a large sum of money, the betrothal contract, and a skin of wine. If the bridal price was approved, a glass of wine was poured and the betrothal contract became a legal document between the two. Though they were now only betrothed, and not yet married, they were considered husband and wife at this time. They were to remain faithful to each other.

In Genesis 24:53, the servant Eliezer went to Rebekah's house with jewels of silver and gold as well as clothing for her. He also gave gifts to her mother and brother. When her family asked if she would go with him to marry Isaac, she gladly agreed (Gen. 24:58). The bridal price was established, and they became betrothed though not officially married yet.

The Bible contains both our betrothal contract as well as our wedding document, known as the *ketubah*. In 1 Corinthians 6:20 we are told we have been bought with a price. Peter tells us just how high the cost was. It was a whole lot more than any corruptible thing, like silver and gold, he said. The price Messiah paid was His own blood (1 Peter 1:18–19)! Messiah also gave gifts to us (Eph. 4:7–8), including spiritual gifts (1 Cor. 12:1).

Within these legal documents the promises of the groom and the rights of the bride are also stated, and 2 Corinthians 1:20 tells us that all the promises of God are yes and amen! We find the rights of the bride in 1 John, which says that we can have what we ask for if we ask according to His will (1 John 5:14–15). But as just Israel, in Exodus, had to give their "I do," so must we. With our mouths, says Romans 10:10, "confession is made to salvation. I find it fascinating that Rebekah gave her "I do" without ever seeing Isaac, and we must give ours as well without having seen Messiah.

Concerning Israel, we find in Hosea that the Lord says He is betrothed to her (Hos. 2:19–20). This betrothal took place at Sinai when they entered into the covenant and said their "I do" (Ex. 19:8; 24:1–8). The problem is, they did not remain faithful and quickly broke the covenant by worshipping a golden calf. The covenant then had to be renewed, and the wedding took place after Moses descended from Mount Sinai on Yom Kippur with a new set of tablets, and immediately they built the tabernacle, or the chuppah, for the bride and groom. There is an amazing connection between the story of the marriage between Isaac and Rebekah and the marriage of God and Israel at Sinai.

Genesis 24:22 says that Eliezer gave Rebekah a golden earring of half a shekel weight. The Hebrew word there for half a shekel is the word *beka*. This is a very unique Hebrew word, as it appears only one other time in the Torah, in Exodus 38:26. God did not want the people to be numbered, so they had to give a half shekel as a ransom for their soul (Ex. 30:12). According to the text in Exodus 38, the half shekel of silver, speaking of redemption, was used for the building of the sockets of the sanctuary and the sockets of the veil in the tabernacle. It says there was a beka per head for the offering. In other words, a beka, or a half shekel, per person is what was offered. The Hebrew word for "head" here is the word *gulgolet*, from which we get the word Golgotha. Being the word for a half shekel, the word *beka* means "to cleave" or "to be broken." In Matthew 27:33, we come to the place of the skull, known as Golgotha. So, according to the Torah, Israel offered up "one broken at Golgotha" for the purpose of building the sanctuary where a sacrificial offering would be accepted for the redemption of their souls! Comparing these Scriptures, we find Isaac had his servant give his bride a golden beka as a wedding gift, similar to the ring given in marriage, now tied to the bride giving the groom a silver ring for the building of the house for the bride and groom.

The Jewish bride would also immerse herself in water, called a *mikvah*, as an act of separation representing that a new life has begun. Now that she had been bought with a price, she would spend the betrothal time learning how to please her husband and await his return as he finished preparing a place for her, just as we see in John 14:1–4, where Yeshua promised to return after building a place for us. Followed by a shout "Blessed is he who comes," the bridegroom would return and the shofar was blown. We see this in the parable of the wise and foolish virgins where it says a cry was made that the bridegroom is coming (Matt. 25:6). This is the shout of Yom Teruah, accompanied by the blowing of the shofar, for the wedding ceremony is about to begin! The bridegroom would abduct his bride and take her to the bridal chamber, where the marriage was consummated.

It is amazing to me that many believers do not want to attend the dress rehearsal of the wedding supper of the Lamb. Yet in Matthew 22, where Yeshua likened the kingdom of heaven to a king who made a marriage for his son, when he sent his servants to call those who had been sent personal invitations to the wedding, they would not come. So he sent more servants, telling those personally invited that the steaks were coming off the grill. Everything was ready, so would they please come to the marriage? Instead, they made light of it and went on their way, more concerned with the things of the world and with making a dollar. Finally, the king says that those who were initially invited were no longer worthy. So the servants were commissioned to invite all they could find, and they were to include the bad with the good so the wedding would be furnished with guests (Matt. 22:1–11).

Similarly, in Luke Yeshua told about a man who made a great supper and invited many (Luke 14:16–24). But as dinnertime rolled around, they had not come. The servant then went to round them up, saying that dinner was ready, but all of them began to make excuses for why they couldn't come. Finally, the master says that none of those who were initially bidden would taste of his supper.

Let me suggest something to you. Many believers today aren't even aware of God's divinely appointed dress rehearsals. When they are made aware, if they make light of their personal invitation, begin to make excuses, and won't even take the time to attend the dress rehearsal, do you think they will respond when the real call comes? The Hebrew word *moed*, translated as "feast," implies meeting at a stated, fixed time based on agreement beforehand. If two people want to get married, they'd better agree on what day and time they plan to do it! In our case, God leads the dance, not us! If you won't agree to His calendar, how in the world do you ever *plan* to meet with Him? Is He to come at *your* beck and call?

Revelation 19 speaks of the marriage supper of the Lamb, and how His wife has made herself ready. She is arrayed in fine linen, clean and white. The text says that those who are called to the marriage supper are blessed (vv. 7–9). Interestingly, the text then mentions the "supper of the Great God." An angel cries out to the fowls of the air to come to this great supper, that they may eat the flesh of kings, captains, and mighty men (vv. 17–18). Which side of the table would you prefer to be on? It's up to you which supper you want to attend.

Psalm 102 says that God will arise and have mercy on Zion. We know Zion is another name for Jerusalem. It goes on to say that the "set time" to favor her has come. The Hebrew word for "set time" is *moed*—a divine appointment! The text continues, "When the LORD shall build up Zion, he shall appear in his glory" (vv. 13, 16). Consider what is going on in the news today! The whole world is upset because of the building up of settlements around Jerusalem. In 1967 Israel recaptured Jerusalem, and ever since the Lord has been building up Zion! It is time for Him to appear in His glory. The next verses declare that this would be written for the generation to come (v. 18). Well, guess what? The Hebrew word for "generation to come" means the terminal or last generation! So the generation that sees the building up of Jerusalem would also be the one that sees the Lord coming in His glory!

We need to realize that there are multiple facets to reality and the things of God. But the problem is that many of us think with a Greek mind-set: there can be only one answer. In the Hebrew mind-set there can be multiple answers. As a matter of fact, it is taught that there are seventy facets to the Scriptures, so just how deep do you want to go in the revelations from God?[3]

To conclude this teaching on Rosh Hashanah, let's recap what we have learned: This feast is also known as the Feast of Trumpets, or Yom Teruah, which means the "Day of Blowing," when the shofar is blown one hundred times. It is blown both to announce the coronation of the King and to serve as the alarm clock at the resurrection of the dead, to awake those who are asleep in the dust of the earth. The shofar also signals the beginning of the "time of trouble," or the Day of Judgment, where the books are opened.

Rosh Hashanah is additionally known as both the day of the wedding of the Messiah and the hidden day. It is very important to remember that while all of these events will happen on this day in *some* year, I am also not saying they will all occur in the *same* year.

One final thing to remember is that when the Lord spoke to Moses concerning the "feasts of the LORD," He meant exactly that: they are the *Lord's* feasts. He even reiterated it by saying, "These are my feasts," which the people were to "proclaim" to be holy dress rehearsals (Lev. 23:1–2). To "proclaim" literally means to call those who have been bidden.

My goal in writing this book is to accomplish that very task. *You* have been invited to the party. Would you please come?

7

THE FEAST OF YOM KIPPUR

In this chapter we will look at the next exciting divine appointment, which also happens to be the most important day of the entire year: Yom Kippur, or the Day of Atonement. We will learn both what that day meant historically, as well as what it might portend for the future, being a dress rehearsal. Scripturally, it was known as Yom Kippurim, or the day of atonements. Why is it in the plural? We find in the book of Leviticus that, though Aaron offered a bull specifically to atone for himself and his house, atonement also had to be made for the holy sanctuary, the tabernacle, the altar, the priests, *and* all the people of the congregation (16:6, 33). All of this has great implications, which we will shortly discover.

So, how was the Day of Atonement different from Passover, you may wonder. Why did God institute Yom Kippur anyway, and how come He had Yeshua die on Passover instead of Yom Kippur? We'll answer these questions momentarily but let me start with the facts. The three fall feasts are all within a couple of weeks of each other. Rosh Hashanah is on the first day of the seventh month and is a reminder that we need to repent by Yom Kippur, which comes shortly thereafter. God set aside a specific day on His calendar for this very special Day of Atonement: the tenth day of the seventh month (Lev. 23:27). So we have a day of repentance, then a short window of time leading to a day of redemption, followed by a day of rejoicing called the Feast of Tabernacles, a weeklong party beginning on the fifteenth day of the seventh month, or Tishri.

Do you remember what happened on the very first Yom Kippur? It followed Israel's worship of the golden calf, after Moses went up the mountain again to make intercession for them (Ex. 32:30–33). Moses told the people they had sinned a great sin, but that he would go up to try and make atonement. He even requested that God would blot him out of the book if that's what it would take to atone for their sin. When Moses came down from Mount Sinai with the two new tablets in his hands, his face was shining so much that the children of Israel were afraid to even come close (Ex. 34:29–30). It was the tenth day of the seventh month, Yom Kippur. On that day Moses declared that God had forgiven them, and they were to take an offering from among the people, whoever would willingly give of what they had, to build the tabernacle, where God Himself would dwell with them (Ex. 35:4–7).

To answer my earlier question, Yom Kippur was only for Israel, as it was their national Day of Atonement. Exodus 19:6 says that Israel was to be a kingdom of priests and a holy nation. Passover, on the other hand, spoke of *individual* redemption.

God had a plan to redeem the whole world, but He chose Israel to be the nation of priests. They were to atone for themselves on Yom Kippur, just as Aaron the high priest had to first make atonement for himself and his family; then five days later, on the Feast of Tabernacles, they were to make atonement for the nations of the world! In this way after the nation of Israel was atoned for as a kingdom of priests, they could in turn now make atonement for the *rest* of the world.

In Genesis 10, after the flood of Noah, God divided the nations of the earth. There were seventy nations at this time. This was a long time before Israel existed. Yet Deuteronomy 32:8 states that when the Most High divided the nations to their inheritance, He set the bounds of the people "according to number of the children of Israel." How can this be? There *were* no "children of Israel" at this time. Did you ever think that God may have had this all planned out? Exodus 1:5 says that out of the loins of Jacob came seventy souls! And every year on the Feast of Tabernacles, five days after Israel's national Day of Atonement, God told Israel to offer up precisely seventy bulls (Num. 29:13–32)—one for each nation![1]

Imagine that! And the old devil is so smart he gets the nations to come and destroy the very sanctuary that God was using to make atonement for them. It was said that if the nations had only known what was being accomplished for them in the Temple, they would have positioned their armies around it to protect it rather than destroy it. This again is why in Matthew, when it talks of separating the sheep from the goats, it means nations, not individuals (25:31–33).

Leviticus mentions that in the year of Jubilee, it was on Yom Kippur that the trumpet of the Jubilee was to sound and they were to hallow the fiftieth year, proclaiming liberty all throughout the land (25:9–10). It was on Yom Kippur that Aaron would take two goats and present them before the Lord at the door of the tabernacle (Lev. 16:6–11). He would cast two lots: one for the scapegoat and one for the Lord. The goat that the Lord's lot fell on was offered up as a sacrifice. Israel believed it was a good omen if the lot for the Lord came up in the right hand of the priest. The other goat was presented alive to make atonement with him and was to be simply let go into the wilderness. Now, how would you like to have that goat, with all of the nation's sin put on its head, show up in your country! Worse, how would you like it sticking around in your country, or for that matter, coming back into town! Israel decided it was best to just throw it over a cliff and be done with it! Historically, they tied a red sash around one of the horns of the scapegoat and another red sash onto one of the doors of the Temple. It is recorded that many times when they threw the scapegoat over the cliff, the red sash attached to the door of the Temple miraculously turned white, so they knew their sins were forgiven. This was based on Isaiah 1:18, which says that though your sins be as scarlet, they will be as white as snow.

The Talmud records four ominous events that took place forty years before the destruction of the Temple.[2] It is said that suddenly the lot for the Lord would no longer come up in the right hand, the scarlet thread stopped turning white, the westernmost light on the Temple menorah wouldn't stay lit, and the Temple doors would open by themselves! This is absolutely incredible when you consider that these events happened around AD 30, which is also the time of the death of Yeshua the Messiah! Josephus wrote of these events as well.[3] According to him, the doors were made of brass, stood seventy-five feet high, and were extremely heavy, taking twenty men to open them. They even had bolts that were fastened into the floor, which was made up of one large stone. Yet, wrote Josephus, at the sixth hour of the night (midnight), the doors would open by themselves! He also said that while the foolish thought it was a good sign, the learned knew better. They realized that their security was being dissolved and the gate was being opened for the advantage of the enemy! This interpretation was based on Zechariah 11:1: "Open your doors, O Lebanon, that the fire may devour your cedars." (If you remember the Temple was made from the cedars of Lebanon.) Again, Josephus recorded that the timing of this event was the sixth hour of the night during Passover week. Does it come as a big surprise, then, that it was at the sixth hour that Pilate said to the Jews, "Behold your king!"—and they responded, "Away with him . . . Crucify him" (John 19:14–15)?

Remember that liberty was to be proclaimed on Yom Kippur. Now follow closely here: On the biblical calendar, the month before the fall feasts is Elul, known as the month of repentance, which is the time to get ready for the fall feasts. John the Baptist baptized Yeshua on the first of Elul; then He went and spent forty days in the wilderness. Forty days takes you to Yom Kippur! So, it was during that holiday that Yeshua came to Nazareth, stood up to read in the Temple, and quoted Isaiah 61: "The Spirit of the Lord is on me, because he has anointed me to preach the gospel to the poor; he has sent me to heal the brokenhearted, to preach deliverance to the captives, and recovering of sight to the blind, to set at liberty them that are bruised, to preach the acceptable year of the Lord," He said. The Bible tells us that He then closed the book and said, "This day is this Scripture fulfilled." Indeed, on Yom Kippur Yeshua was proclaiming the year of Jubilee (Luke 4:1–2, 14–21). You will not believe what happened next!

"And all they in the synagogue, when they heard these things, were filled with wrath, and rose up, and thrust him out of the city, and led him to the brow of the hill where on their city was built, that they might cast him down headlong." Do you see what I see? Here it was, Yom Kippur, and He was being the scapegoat that the people were ready to throw over the cliff!

But it was not His time yet. Note that as He quoted from the book of Isaiah, He stopped short, midsentence. In Isaiah 61:2, after the phrase "to proclaim the acceptable year of the LORD," it says, "and the day of vengeance of our God." So what does that mean? When Yeshua came, it was only time to proclaim the "acceptable year of the Lord"; the day of vengeance was on hold for the time in which *we* live.

Let's go back for a moment and look again at the Yom Kippur ceremony. Leviticus 16 says that the high priest was to have on the holy linen coat, the linen breeches, a linen girdle, and a linen miter when he did the sacrificial offerings (vv. 3–5). Can you imagine having on all white linen while conducting all kinds of bloody sacrifices? We know from Revelation 19:8 that white linen speaks of righteousness. Can there be any doubt, after going over the Feast of Trumpets, that this, too, is a dress rehearsal? After all, do you hear anything about "trumpets" in the book of Revelation? Of course you do. So now let's go through the yearly Day of Atonement ritual and see if we can find any upcoming rehearsal themes in the book of Revelation.

First, the high priest was to *take a censer of burning coals of fire from off the altar* before the Lord, with his hands full of sweet incense that's been beaten, and bring it into the Holy of Holies (Lev. 16:12–15). He was then to put the incense on the fire so a cloud of incense would cover the mercy seat so he wouldn't die. He then would take the blood of the bull and the blood of the goat and sprinkle each of them seven times on the mercy seat. We know from Scripture that our prayers are likened to incense (Ps. 141:2). Remember also that the tabernacle was patterned after the one in heaven. So there is something happening simultaneously in heaven as it is happening in the tabernacle on earth. Now we go to Revelation.

In Revelation 6, when the fifth seal is opened, John sees under the altar in heaven the souls of those slain for the Word of God and for the testimony they held. Listen to what they cry: "How long, O Lord, holy and true, do you not judge and avenge our blood on them that dwell on the earth?" They want the day of vengeance to begin! Instead, they are given white robes and told to rest awhile (vv. 9–11).

In Revelation 8, we see an angel in heaven with a golden censer who comes and stands by the altar. "And there was given to him much incense, that he should offer it with the prayers of all saints on the golden altar which was before the throne. And the smoke of the incense, which came with the prayers of the saints, ascended up before God out of the angel's hand." The angel *then takes the censer, fills it with fire from the altar*, and casts it to the earth. Then seven angels having seven trumpets prepare to sound them (vv. 3–6). This is exactly what was happening in Leviticus!

To this day, when Yom Kippur is celebrated, all those who attend the service come dressed in white. Even the high priest had to take off his beautiful garments on this day and put on the all-white linen garments that would be stained with the blood from the sacrifices. Now let's go back to Isaiah.

In Isaiah 63, we read, "Who is this that comes from Edom, with dyed garments from Bozrah? . . . Why are you red in your apparel and your garments like him who treads in the winefat?" (vv. 1–2). In other words, his garments are all stained with blood! Messiah says that He alone has treaded the winepress, without any human company. He goes on to say that He will tread them in His anger and trample them in His fury, and their blood shall be sprinkled upon His garments. He will stain *all* His raiment, He says, "for the day of vengeance is in my heart, and the year of my redeemed is come" (vv. 3–4)!

This is truly amazing as we see this is a Yom Kippur event when the Messiah as High Priest comes as our Kinsman-Redeemer, the blood avenger to avenge the blood of the inno-cent—including the souls under the altar in Revelation!

Notice He is treading the winepress. The fall feasts are in the seventh month, which is the time of the grape harvest. This is why the angel in Revelation 14:18 was told to thrust in his "sharp sickle, and gather the clusters of the vine of the earth; for her grapes are fully ripe." God wanted to make this so simple for us, and we so greatly complicate it by all our dogmas. Yeshua plainly said in Matthew that the field in His parable was the world, the good seed are the children of the kingdom, and the tares are the children of the wicked one (13:38–39). Then He said that the enemy who sowed the tares is the devil, the harvest is the end of the world, and the reapers are the angels. This is why all the feasts are harvest feasts. So we would get it! Ancient Israel was a farming-based society. This is why in Exodus God told Israel that three times in the year they were to appear before Him at His appointed times: in the first month for the barley harvest and the Feast of Unleavened Bread; then for the Feast of Shavuot, celebrating the wheat harvest in the third month; then also for the feast of ingathering, which is at the end of the year, speaking of the grape harvest (Ex. 23:14-16). Now for a moment, let's return to Isaiah.

In Isaiah 63:3, remember that Messiah was all alone as He was having His garments stained; none of the people were with Him. If we compare this to the ceremony on the Day of Atonement, we find that no one was allowed in the tabernacle of the congregation from the time the high priest went in to make atonement in the holy place, until he came out and had atoned for himself, his household, and all the congregation of Israel (Lev. 16:17). Similarly, in Revelation 15:8, when the Temple was filled with the smoke of God's glory and power, "no man was able to enter into the temple.

Do you see the Day of Yom Kippur now in the book of Revelation? Well, there's more! After the seventh angel sounds, the time of God's wrath is come, along with the time of the judging of the dead and the rewarding of the saints (Rev. 11:15–19). As a reminder, on Yom Teruah the heavenly court is in session and God judges everyone. The trial lasts ten days, and on Yom Kippur the books are closed and the sentence is meted out, whether good or bad. Here we see this time frame again as God sits in judgment and hands out rewards. Only once a year could the high priest enter into the Holy of Holies and come before the ark of the covenant (Lev. 16:2, 34). The next verse in Revelation says the "temple of God was opened in heaven, and there was seen in his temple the ark of his testament: and there were lightning, and voices, and thunders, and an earthquake, and great hail" (Rev. 11:20). If you don't think this is a Yom Kippur event, I don't know what to say!

So let's continue in Revelation 19, and what do we find concerning the time frame from the Feast of Trumpets to Yom Kippur? I will summarize some verses in chapter 19 for you. It says, "For true and righteous are [Messiah's] judgments; for he has judged the great whore . . . and has avenged the blood of his servants at her hand!" (v. 2). It goes on to say He is clothed with a vesture dipped in blood, and His name is called the Word of God. The armies that follow Him are riding on white horses, and they all are clothed in fine linen, white and clean! Hello! Yom Kippur! Everyone is wearing white! Finally, it states that out of His mouth is a sharp sword with which He will smite the nations, and He will rule them with a rod of iron and tread the winepress of the fierceness and wrath of Almighty God (vv. 13–15)!

The Hebrew word for atonement meant "to cover," There's a couple of ways that I like to describe the term. One is by thinking of something that covers over an offense or covers for an offense. For instance, in Genesis, when Abraham gave Sarah over to Abimelech and then God threatened him in a dream, Abimelech told Sarah he had given Abraham a thousand pieces of silver as a "covering" of the eyes to all that were with her (Gen. 20:16). His money *atoned* for the offense. In Proverbs, on the other hand, in speaking of adultery, it says there is no amount of ransom money that will atone for the aggrieved husband (Prov. 6:35). The idea behind atonement was to offer a gift to make an offense right and have a relationship restored.

Psalm 49:7 speaks of how no one can redeem, or atone for, a soul with money. The psalm goes on to say, "God [is the One who] will redeem my soul (v. 15). Similarly, Galatians 3:13 says that Messiah is the one who redeemed us.

Only one person could go into the Holy of Holies and survive, and even that one could enter only once a year, and that was on Yom Kippur. Consequently, this feast also came to be known as Face to Face. In Ezekiel 20 it is prophesied that God will rule over Israel when He gathers them out of the countries where they have been scattered. He will bring them into the wilderness, and there He will plead with them "face to face" (vv. 33–35). I believe the prophet was telling us this event will happen some year on the feast of Yom Kippur.

In Hosea we find a very interesting prophecy. I can't help but think of Yeshua and the destruction of the Temple in AD 70 when I read it. It says, "I will go and return to my place, till they acknowledge their offense, and seek my face: in their affliction they will seek me early. Come, and let us return to the LORD: for he has torn, and he will heal us; he has smitten, and he will bind us up." (Hos. 5:15–6:2). Now remember: the Bible states that a day with the Lord is as a thousand years (Ps. 90:4). Hosea goes on to say, "After two days will he revive us: in the third day he will raise us up, and we shall live in his sight" (Hos. 6:3)! This is incredible! After two thousand years, or "two days," Israel *was* revived and came back to life. The "third day" is the third millennium, when the resurrection of the dead takes place and they live in His sight! We are in the third millennium now! Anytime, we could be living in Yeshua's sight!

Then Hosea says we will finally understand that He comes as the rain, "as the latter and former rain on the earth" (v. 4). These spring and fall rains are related to the spring and fall feasts! The spring feasts consummated His first coming, and His second coming will be by the fall feasts.

I believe God was speaking of a Yom Kippur event when He said, "I will pour on the house of David, and on the inhabitants of Jerusalem, the spirit of grace and of supplications: and they shall look on me whom they have pierced, and they shall mourn for him, as one mourns for his only son" (Zech. 12:10). I believe this day is set aside prophetically for the nation of Israel. Of course, I must say there is a veil over all nations. Isaiah wrote that God will destroy the face of the covering that is cast over all people and the veil that is over all nations (Isa. 25:7). The veil is opened on Yom Kippur! Listen to the next verse as well, considering the timing. It says, "He will swallow up death in victory; and the Lord GOD will wipe away tears from off all faces" (v. 8a). This is where Revelation 21:4 comes from! Revelation 21 continues by saying, "He that sat on the throne said, Behold, I make all things new." Then He told John to write that these words are true and faithful (vv. 5–6)! Do you see all the dots connecting here yet? The Feast of Trumpets is the day the heavenly court is in session, the Judge is on the throne, and the books are opened. At the end of Yom Kippur, the books are closed and judgment is meted out. Then come new beginnings! First John is writing in a book; then God is sitting on His throne, and ultimately even death itself is judged, as it says in 1 Corinthians: "In a moment, in the twinkling of an eye, at the last trump: for the trumpet shall sound, and the dead shall be raised incorruptible. . . . Then shall be brought to pass the saying that is written, Death is swallowed up in victory. O death, where is your sting? O grave, where is your victory?" (15:52, 54–55). Then all things become new, exactly what happens on Yom Kippur. It is at this time that the rebuke of God's people—the nation of Israel—will be taken away from off all the earth (Isa. 25:8b).

But for now, all nations are blinded to the Messiah. Even we Christians "see through a glass, darkly" but the time is coming when we too shall see face to face (1 Cor. 13:12)! Some year, on Yom Kippur, or Face to Face, a divinely appointed day predetermined in history, we, too, will fully understand.

As we move to the next chapter and look at probably my favorite feast, the Feast of Tabernacles, I want to close with this thought from the book of Acts. Again, Paul was saying to the brethren that he didn't want them to be ignorant. He explained to them that everything God foretold by the mouths of the prophets regarding how Messiah would suffer, Yeshua fulfilled it. Remember that at the time Acts was written, Yeshua had already come, risen, and ascended to heaven. So now Paul was telling them what has to happen before Yeshua can be sent back. He said that if they would repent, then times of refreshing would come from the presence of the Lord. Then He would send Yeshua, "whom the heavens must receive until the times of the restitution of all things," which God spoke through the prophets since the world began (Acts 3:18–21). Do you realize what this is saying? It is saying that Yeshua will not come back until everything is restored that the prophets spoke of *from the very beginning*, not just since the book of Acts! One item that needs to be restored is God's calendar!

To sum up the teaching about the Feast of Yom Kippur, remember that this is Israel's national Day of Atonement. In the next chapter, about the Feast of Tabernacles, you will learn that it is also known as the Feast of the Nations. In God's overall plan to reconcile mankind after the fall in the Garden, He chose a man, Abraham, from whom God would form a nation in a way that had never existed before. This nation would be a kingdom of priests who were to intercede and make atonement for the nations of the world after themselves being cleansed on their Day of Atonement. Five days later, during the Feast of Tabernacles, they would slay the seventy bulls, one for each nation. This would happen every year as a dress rehearsal until the time of the fulfillment of God's redemptive plan. Historically, the adversary has done everything in his power to prevent this from happening. All of mankind, in their jealousy, pride, and arrogance regarding who plays what role, if any, in their own mind, has kept this from happening.

Fortunately, we know that God's plans are never thwarted, and His will will be done in His time. So the question then becomes: how should Christians celebrate Yom Kippur? Remember, you can always go to our website and watch our archived live stream service for ideas. Simply do what you can do with just your family or friends. If your church wants more info on the how-tos, then contact our office. But study what it is all about and research what you can. Yom Kippur is a biblical fast day, so everyone fasts. Our services are the night before, and traditionally everyone comes wearing white that evening, as white represents righteousness. During the service our focus is on the holiness of God and His thirteen attributes. We worship and teach about what Yom Kippur is all about. We pray for the nation of Israel, that they would return to the Torah and fulfill their role that God has assigned to them. Then we leave in awe as we set apart the Day of Yom Kippur.

As I said earlier, there are many events that will happen on the Feast of Trumpets but not all in the same year. I do believe there will be partial fulfillments of all three feasts in one year, though, as there were for the spring feasts. As far as an order goes, I believe the next feast to be fulfilled on the prophetic calendar is the Feast of Trumpets, giving warning that the last week of the seven years of Jacob's trouble has begun. Then, in some year following will be fulfilled Israel's Day of Atonement, where they will see God face to face. Finally, some year following that will be the fulfillment of the next feast, the Feast of Tabernacles, when the Messiah tabernacles among men for a thousand years! I don't know if you are excited yet, but I sure am! Let's jump right into our next divine appointment!

THE FEAST OF TABERNACLES

This feast has to be my favorite! Wait till you see all the nuggets buried in this one. Talk about buried treasure! There are so many found at so many different levels it is beyond imagination. So let's dig in!

This preordained divine appointment penciled in God's day timer from the foundation of the world is celebrated for a whole week! The party begins on the fifteenth day of the seventh month, Tishri. We find its introduction in Leviticus. God told Moses that Israel was to have a party and celebrate for seven days every year as a statute forever (Lev. 23:41–43). God actually commanded them to rejoice the entire time. Whoever calls this legalism is out of their minds. Imagine it: God saying, "No whining for seven whole days"! No wonder the legalists can't handle it! Three times in the text they were told to dwell in booths, or temporary shelters, during the festival, mainly because God made them dwell in booths in the wilderness after He brought them out of Egyptian slavery.

This is why the Feast of Tabernacles is also known as the Feast of Booths. The words *tabernacle* and *booth* both carry the same concept. The Hebrew word for *booths* is *sukkot*, its traditional name. Other names for this festival include: the

Feast of Ingathering, the Season of our Joy, and, as mentioned earlier, the Feast of Nations. So where do we start? First let me ask you a question.

Do you believe God is the same yesterday, today, and forever (Heb. 13:8)? If so, what does that actually mean to you? James wrote that in God there is not even a *shadow* of turning (James 1:17). Yet many believers think God changes His mind at the turn of a dial, especially when it comes to keeping the biblical feasts. But let's look for a moment at a passage from the book of Zechariah.

In Zechariah 14 the prophet wrote that the day of the Lord is coming, when every nation will gather against Jerusalem to battle. Messiah Himself will return, His feet landing on and splitting in two the Mount of Olives, and He will battle the nations. After this ultimate battle, He will be the one Lord and King over all the earth (Zech. 14:1–9). Do you see all the imagery of the fall feasts in this text? Judgment is coming, the King is on His throne, and the nations must submit or consequences will come.

Zechariah goes on to say that Jerusalem will be the safe place to be, even during a replay of the plagues in Egypt. The wealth of the nations will be gathered together for Israel, all the gold, silver, and apparel in great abundance, just as in the Exodus story (14:10–15).

Now comes the big revelation! *Every year* for the next one thousand years, everyone who is left of the nations that came against Jerusalem has to go up and worship the King, the Lord of hosts, and keep the Feast of Tabernacles (14:16–19)! As a matter of fact, it is stated *three times* for emphasis. All the nations have to keep the Feast of Tabernacles, or else they get the plague and no rain! The choice is theirs!

So tell me, if God *is* the same yesterday, today, and forever, would He command that the Feast of Tabernacles, which He designed Himself, be kept, but then say it was a dumb idea of His? Would He change His mind, then curse Israel if they tried to follow His command—and then turn around and say He was wrong *again*, the feast is now good again after all, so every nation has to keep it or He plagues them? That sounds like a schizophrenic God with some real anger issues. That's not the God I serve, but that is the God many religious leaders serve up. They say the Feast of the LORD were once good, now they are done away with. Oh, but now it looks like they are good again! Will they tell Yeshua they aren't coming to His feast because He's being legalistic? He does give them that choice.

The Feast of Tabernacles was one of three pilgrimage feasts, when the people were to come to Jerusalem and, for a time, dwell with God there. (Ex. 23:14–17; Deut.16:16). God's ultimate plan from the foundation of the world has always been to dwell, or tabernacle, with His people. He did tabernacle with one young couple, Adam and Eve, for a very short time in the garden of Eden, but because of disobedience, it abruptly ended. Then, around twenty-five hundred years later, He tried it again, but this time with a nation. In Exodus God told Moses to allow Israel to make a sanctuary, that He might dwell within them (25:8–9). And coincidentally, they began to build the tabernacle at the time of the Feast of Tabernacles (Ex. 35:20–22).

It's important to realize that Moses had to make the tabernacle after the pattern God had showed him. There is also a heavenly tabernacle, where the events echoed on earth are being performed in heaven.

Tragically, due to disobedience, the glory departed from Israel. The good news is that God will once again tabernacle among mankind in Jerusalem (Ezek. 43:1–4; Rev. 21:3).

Why did God insist that Israel dwell in tabernacles, or temporary dwelling places, every year throughout all their generations as an eternal statute? God wanted to remind us all, each year at this appointed time, that both the earth and our mortal bodies are also only temporary dwelling places. This is why we read in both Isaiah 51:6 and Hebrews that the heavens will vanish as smoke and the earth will wax old like a garment and all flesh will go in like manner (Heb. 1:10–12). But the apostle Paul wrote in 2 Corinthians 5:1 that when our earthly house of this tabernacle is dissolved, there's one waiting for us in the heavens, built by God. The Greek word for tabernacle is *skenos* (σκηνος). This is referring to the human body, which is taken down at death much as you would take down a tent after a camping trip. And the word *tabernacle* in reference to our body connects us to the concept of the Feast of Tabernacles.

Peter wrote that as long as he was in his "tabernacle," he wanted to remind everyone of the truth, because Yeshua had shown him in advance that he would soon "put off" his tabernacle, referring to his death (2 Peter 1:12–16). The context of this statement is exciting, as Peter went on to state that they had not been following cunningly devised fables when they had made known the power and coming of the Lord Jesus Christ, but that they had been eyewitnesses of His majesty. *When* had Peter and his friends become eyewitnesses to the power and coming of the Messiah?

In the gospel of Mark, Yeshua told His disciples that some of them would not die until they had a chance to see the kingdom of God come with power (9:1–7). Six days later, Yeshua took Peter, James, and John to a high mountain and was transfigured before them. Peter saw Moses and Elijah alongside Yeshua as well at His coming in power. Notice that the first thing Peter asked is if he should make three tabernacles. Have you ever asked yourself why Peter would say that? Because this event took place during the Feast of Tabernacles![1]

The requirement to rejoice for seven days comes from Leviticus, which lays out some of the specifics for the festival. As mentioned earlier, it was to begin on the fifteenth day of Tishri, when Israel had gathered in the fruit of the land. The first day was to be a Sabbath, as was the eighth day (Lev. 23:39–40). Wahoo! Who wouldn't want to rejoice with an eight-day party, including two extra days off work within a two-week period, to spend time with friends from all over the world and rejoice with our Maker?

In 2 Chronicles we read about the dedication of Solomon's Temple, which just so happened to be during the feasts of the seventh month (5:1–14). This was perfect timing for an inauguration ceremony, because everyone was required to be there anyway. Plus, they wanted to be there. Can you imagine the festivities, with hundreds of thousands of people all rejoicing together over a full week? We read that 120 priests came out of the holy place with trumpets to join the Levites, who were all arrayed in white linen, singing praises to the Lord with cymbals, psalteries (stringed instruments), and harps. Then—bam!—the glory fell! The next several chapters go on to detail Solomon's dedicatory prayer, when fire fell from heaven. The people kept the Feast of Tabernacles all the way through the eighth day, having a solemn assembly (2 Chron. 7:1–9).

According to Josephus, during the time of Yeshua, over two million people would be in Jerusalem for the feasts.[2] The pilgrims were coming to rejoice and celebrate in the temple! And according to the Talmud, Jewish writings about these times:

> Rabbi Yehoshua ben Chanina said: During the days of the water libation ceremony, we barely got to sleep at all. The first hour of the day saw us attending to the daily offering; following this we were engaged in prayer—afterwards, the additional offering. Then we ate, and it already became time to attend to the afternoon service, and this was followed by the celebration of the festival of the water libation, which lasted the entire night, and we would begin again.[3]

We also find in other writings that as the people sang, men juggling flaming torches would dance before them. Two priests blowing silver trumpets would stand at the top of the stairs on either side of the entrance to the great gate of the court, while the singers stood on the fifteen steps, playing all kinds of other musical instruments.[4] There are so many significant details I will expand on later, but let me give you one more historical tidbit concerning the Feast of Tabernacles. The Talmud mentions four enormous candlesticks with four golden bowls at the top of each in the women's court. They were about seventy five feet high, with their wicks made from worn-out priestly garments, cut into strips. Four young priests would climb to the top, carrying immense oil jugs to fill the bowls. It was said that once lighted, there was not a courtyard in all of Jerusalem that did not glow with the light emanating from the celebration in the Temple courtyard.[5] Men, women, and children all participated in the immense joy of the water libation. Special elevated balconies were constructed in the women's court to enable the women to watch the men of the Sanhedrin as they danced.

You have to remember that at this feast, Jerusalem was known as the light of the world. It was during this feast that Yeshua stood up and declared that He was the Light of the World (John 8:12)! There were so many pilgrims at the feast that all twenty-four courses of priests would serve during the week.

One of the last things David accomplished before he passed was to divide the Levitical priests into twenty-four "courses" (1 Chron. 23:27–32). Each course would serve one week twice a year (24:1–18), for a total of forty-eight weeks, and then the remaining three weeks of the annual lunar cycle, all the priests would serve for the pilgrimage festivals of Passover, Pentecost, and Tabernacles because there would be so many people there for the festivities.

I think it funny that only the men were required to be there, but the women and children weren't. Maybe it was because God knew that women love to socialize, so they would come anyway. The men, on the other hand, had to be told what to do because if it were up to them, they probably would have stayed home and worked on the farm!

During the Feast of Tabernacles, the twenty-four courses of priests were divided into three groups to conduct the daily ceremonies. One group would be responsible for the slaying of all the daily sacrifices. A second group conducted the daily water libation ceremony. Headed by the high priest, they would go through the Water Gate, down to the pool of Siloam, because it held "living water." The high priest would draw this living water from the pool with a golden vase. His assistant held a silver vase filled with wine. Imagine the thousands of spectators forming a pathway as these priests ascended again up to the Temple. When they reached the Water Gate, they blew a sustained, a quavering, and another sustained blast on the shofar. Once back at the altar, they would pour out the water and the "blood" of the grapes into special silver bowls in the corner of the altar. The wine was poured slowly and the water quickly. The bowl on the west was for the water and the one on the east was for the wine. (One time during the celebrations, a priest who didn't care for the whole ceremony poured the water at his feet and was stoned with etrogs, or citrus fruit!⁶) Prayers for blessing on earth were accompanied with prayers for rain so the winter crops would be plentiful. (Remember, they were in a desert climate.) Every day they would march around the altar, singing from the Psalms. Of course they would sing the Hallel, which is Psalms 113–118. Among the lyrics they would sing during the Feast of Tabernacles are these, from Psalm 118: "The LORD is my strength and song, and is become my salvation. The voice of rejoicing and salvation is in the tabernacles of the righteous: the right hand of the LORD does valiantly" (vv. 14–15). This refers to the salvation Israel experienced at the Red Sea when Moses, Miriam, and all the children of Israel sang unto the Lord the very same words (Ex. 15:1–2). The Exodus passage goes on to say that, "He is my God, and I will prepare him an habitation." This is why to this very day every religious Jew around the world and especially in Israel builds a booth, or sukkah, in which to spend time rejoicing during this week.

On the last day of the feast, Israel would do a Jericho march around the altar seven times during the pouring out of the water and the wine. Again they would be singing the Hallel.

Now here comes another one of the most amazing discoveries

in the New Testament for those connected to the deep roots of their faith. It was during this feast that Yeshua's brothers told Him to make Himself known, as they hadn't really believed in Him yet. Yeshua said it was not the right time (John 7:1–8). But then Yeshua did something incredible. Can you imagine if, right in the middle of worship during one of your church services, someone jumped up and started crying out, "You're singing about me"? That is exactly what happened in John 7:37. It says that on the last day of the feast, Yeshua stood and cried out, "If any man thirst, let him come to me, and drink. He that believes on me, as the scripture has said, out of his belly shall flow rivers of living water." What scripture was He referring to? According to Jewish tradition, the people would also sing Isaiah 12 because it also repeats the phrase "the LORD . . . is my strength and my song . . . [and] is become my salvation" (v. 12). I believe it was right in the middle of their singing Isaiah 12 that Yeshua cried out with everything He had, because the next verse says, "Therefore with joy shall you draw water out of the wells of salvation." The word *salvation* in Hebrew in this verse is *Yeshua,* which is Messiah's name *Yeshua*! So the moment they sang, "With joy shall you draw water out of the wells of Yeshua," He cried out, "You are singing about Me! As the Scripture says, *I* am the well of living water; come and drink!" What is just breathtaking is how they finished the song from Isaiah 12 after Yeshua cried out in their midst. Imagine the scene again as they uttered these final words: "Cry out and shout, you inhabitant of Zion: for great is the Holy One of Israel in your midst" (v. 6). There He was, standing amidst them and crying out to them, as they themselves were singing the command to cry out to the Holy One in their midst! Incredible!

The third group of priests during the Feast of Tabernacles would go out the Beautiful Gate heading to the Motza Valley, and there they would cut down willow branches about twenty feet in length. A parade of priests would march in rows back up to the Beautiful Gate, waving the willow branches. The people, too, would cut willow branches, and they would stand them up around the altar so the heads would be bent about two feet above the altar. You can almost hear the leaves rustling on the thousands of willows being shaken in the wind. The Hebrew word for wind is *ruach*, which is also translated as "spirit." So from the south, toward the Temple, a mass of people and priests came bearing the "living water" and the "blood" toward the Water Gate. From the east, heading up toward the Beautiful Gate, was another mass of people, all marching in unison while shaking willow branches bringing the "wind of the Spirit" toward the Temple. When they got to their respective gates, they would stop and wait for the sound of a priest playing a flute. According to Jewish history a flutist would always play during the week of Sukkot, or the Feast of Tabernacles.[7] As a flute is pierced, he was known as "the pierced one," calling for the Spirit and living water to enter the temple.

In John 7, after Yeshua had cried out, many of the people believed that He must be the prophet that Moses had predicted would come; others believed He was the Christ (John 7:40–41). But the Pharisees told them they were *all* deceived! And worse, they said, "This people who knows not the law are cursed" (v. 49)! The truth is, it was the *Pharisees* who knew not the law. So who were the cursed ones? These Pharisees remind me of our own government leaders, who mandate all sorts of laws to us, but don't know or follow the Constitution themselves! I guess not much has changed in two thousand years.

You are probably familiar with the Lord's statement, "Behold, I stand at the door, and knock: if any man hear my voice, and open the door, I will come in to him, and will sup with him, and he with me" (Rev. 3:20). Remember that this verse was written not to an individual, but to a church (v. 14). The Lord is standing outside the door, knocking, asking the church to open the door. The people are all inside, having church, and don't even realize the Lord isn't there! When He asks them to let Him in, they don't recognize Him. Their response is essentially, "Leave us alone; we're having church!"

In Jeremiah 2, God is reprimanding the priests when He says that the very ones who handle the Law don't even know Him (v. 8)! God goes on to say that His people have committed two evils: first, He says, "they have forsaken me the fountain of living waters"; and second, they have hewed out "broken cisterns, that can hold no water." Remember that in John 7, Yeshua invited all who were thirsty to drink and to believe in Him. Only He can provide living water (vv. 37–38). Sadly, the religious leaders, who were supposed to know the law, forsook Him, *the* Living Water— just like the priests in Jeremiah's day—on the last day of the Feast of Tabernacles, when He was tabernacling *in their very midst*.

The eighth day of the Feast of Tabernacles is known as Simchat Torah, or Rejoicing in the Torah. It is also called Shemini Atzeret, or in English, the Eighth Day of Assembly. The Feast of Tabernacles itself was seven days, but God added this additional, eighth day as a Sabbath to end the feast. On this day the people were to just rest in God and rejoice in the fact that He had given them the Torah.

Interestingly, in John 8, it was that eighth day, Simchat Torah (vv. 1–2). After spending the night on the Mount of Olives in the sukkah He had built for the feast, Yeshua returned to the Temple, and as the people came to Him, He, befittingly, sat down and taught them. What a concept! Yeshua, the Living Torah, teaching Torah in the Temple on the very day everyone was meant to rejoice in it.

But what happened next? The Pharisees came back, and instead of rejoicing in the Torah, they mishandled it and used this very day of rejoicing to condemn someone to death! They brought to Yeshua a woman caught in the act of adultery—the very act, mind you! Then, sarcastically calling Him "Master," they tested Him to see if they could find some reason to accuse Him of breaking the Torah. "Now Moses in the law commanded us, that such should be stoned," they told Him, "but what say *you*?" (John 8:5; emphasis added).

Yeshua played their game—and He caught them in their own "Moses trap." If anybody knows the law, Yeshua does!

The law states that if a false witness rises up to testify falsely against someone, then both of them have to stand before the Lord, and before the priests and judges in place at the time. The judges are to "make diligent inquisition" to get all the facts, just as in a modern court. If the false witness is discovered to be a liar, then what was supposed to happen to the accused will become the punishment meted out to the one giving the false testimony (Deut. 19:16–19). The law also states that both the adulterous woman *and* the man are to be put to death (Lev. 20:10). So my question is, if she was caught in the *very act* . . . where was the man? Let's hear his testimony! What's more, where were the witnesses? Was she just handed over to a mob? Where was her husband? Or, was she, in fact, raped? Time for a trial!

Seemingly ignoring them, Yeshua stooped down and started writing on the ground. I've often wondered what He was writing in the dirt. Not only that, I wonder where the dirt even came from. I thought the Temple had marble floors. This is why I love reading Jewish history, because it gives us so much missing detail!

The *Halacha*, the collective body of Jewish laws originating from the written and Oral Torah, is the Jews' rule book. (Regardless of whether you consider the Oral Torah to be inspired or not, it has enormous historical value for those wanting to understand what was happening back then. It's a two-thousand-year-old document!) According to the written Torah, when a woman is suspected of adultery, she is supposed to be brought before the priest by her husband! Specifically, the book of Numbers, which is the beginning of the rule book, states that if "the spirit of jealousy" comes upon him, then he is to bring his wife to the priest, and the priest brings her before the Lord. Then the priest is to take holy water in an earthen vessel and add to it some dust from the floor of the tabernacle (Num. 5:12–17). This was written in the time of Moses.

Now, over fifteen hundred years later, Yeshua stood in Herod's temple. According to the Halacha, the *sotah*—that is, the woman suspected of adultery—must go through the trial of bitter waters to see if the accusation against her is true. There is an entire dissertation in the Talmud dealing with this jealousy ordeal, called tractate Sotah.

In Herod's temple, there was a one-cubit-by-one-cubit opening in the floor, to the right as one entered the sanctuary, that was covered by a marble tile with a ring affixed to it. The priest could easily lift the tile and literally "take from the dust of the earth of the tabernacle." I believe this is exactly what Yeshua did in front of the mob.

Back to Numbers and the Sotah, once the suspected woman was set before the Lord, the priest would charge her with an oath and a curse that she should confess whether or not the accusation against her was true. The priest would then write the curse and oath in a book and blot them out with the bitter water containing the holy dust from the tabernacle. The woman would then drink the bitter water that caused the curse. If the woman was innocent, she would be free and could conceive. But if she was guilty, her belly would swell and her thigh would rot (Num. 5:19–29). Then, not only would she die, but her adulterous partner, wherever he was, also died (Lev. 20:10; Deut. 22:22). Incredibly, in the Jewish writings, it is said that during the Second Temple period, adultery was so rampant that the priests stopped administering the bitter waters![8]

All of a sudden, the mob before Yeshua began to get nervous, because what was supposed to happen to the adulterous woman would happen to *them* if they had falsely accused her—or if one of them had been her partner.

Just then, Yeshua stood up and said, "Whoever is without sin cast the first stone." He then started writing on the ground again—while all the accusers walked away totally ashamed. What brought their shame? Had some of them committed adultery in the past? We do know that just the day before, they had rejected Yeshua as the fountain of living waters. And look what Jeremiah had to say about those who forsake "the fountain of living waters": "O LORD, the hope of Israel, all that forsake you shall be ashamed, and they that depart from me shall be *written in the earth*, because they have forsaken the LORD, the fountain of living waters" (Jer. 17:13; emphasis added). In Jeremiah's time, Israel had committed spiritual adultery by forsaking the Lord, and as a result, their names would be "written in the earth." For their own spiritual adultery after rejecting his "living water," could Yeshua have been writing the names of the woman's accusers in the earth? If so, they would have seen them in the dust as He stood up. No wonder they all took off! He had given them a taste of their own medicine!

All of this happened during the Feast of Tabernacles. Because of the command to dwell in booths, during Yeshua's time there would have been thousands of sukkahs surrounding Jerusalem, as well as all throughout the land of Israel. If you remember, Israel first began to build the tabernacle at the Feast of Tabernacles. In John 1:14 we find that "the Word was made flesh, and dwelled among us." The Greek word for "dwelled"— *skenos* (σκηνος), which we looked at earlier—can be translated as "tabernacle," meaning this could be read as "Yeshua tabernacled among us." Let's take a look at Yeshua's birth and see if just maybe He fulfilled the Feast of Tabernacles by being born on the first day of the feast, tabernacling among His creation!

In Luke 1 we learn that in the days of Herod, the king of Judea, a priest named Zacharias, "of the course of Abia," or Abijah, "executed the priest's office before God in the order of his course" (vv. 5, 8). Going back to 1 Chronicles, we read that when David divided the priests, Abijah was in the eighth "lot," or course (24:10). In verse 19 we see that the priests were to come serve in the house of the Lord according to their "orderings."

The religious year begins on Nisan 1, roughly our April 1. Each course would serve one week twice a year, and all the priests would serve during the three pilgrimage weeks: Passover,

Pentecost, and Tabernacles. So, for simplicity's sake, let's use a calendar in which Nisan 1 lines up with our April 1. We'll also line up April/Nisan 1 with the first day of the week, Sunday, for an easier visual as well.

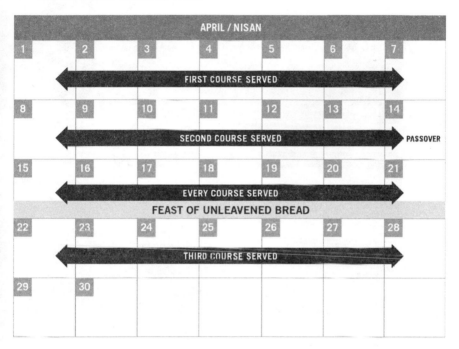

The first week the first course would be served, and the second week the second course would be served. But the third week, being the Feast of Unleavened Bread, every course was served. So the priests serving the second week would have to remain and do another week as well. The priests serving the third week would also be serving two weeks in a row, first during the week of unleavened bread, then an additional week for their own course. Let's go to the next month.

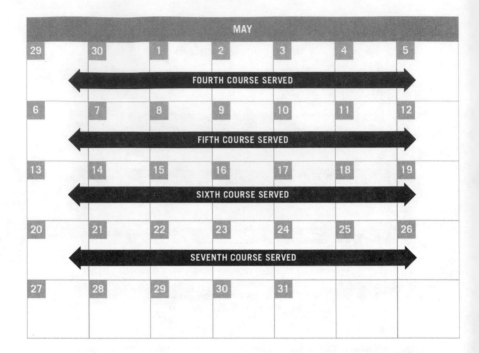

As you can see, the fourth, fifth, sixth, and seventh courses would be served in May, and the eighth course would be served at the end of May and into June.

What do we find? The eighth course of Abijah would have to be served two weeks in a row because they'd also have to stay and serve the week of Pentecost!

In Luke we find that while Zacharias was executing the priest's office before God in the order of his course, according to the custom of the priest's office, his lot was to burn incense when he went into the Temple of the Lord (1:8–11). There were so many priests that there was a lottery system as to who would get to do the different parts of the service each day. You could offer incense only once in your entire life! Zacharias was old and

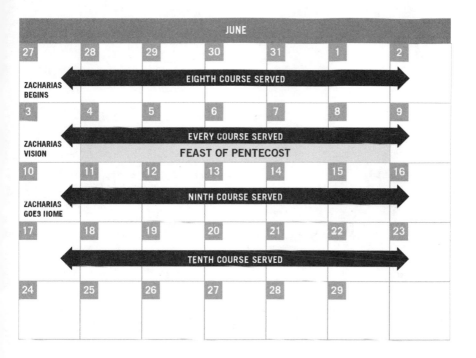

JUNE						
27	28	29	30	31	1	2
ZACHARIAS BEGINS	EIGHTH COURSE SERVED					
3	4	5	6	7	8	9
ZACHARIAS VISION	EVERY COURSE SERVED FEAST OF PENTECOST					
10	11	12	13	14	15	16
ZACHARIAS GOES HOME	NINTH COURSE SERVED					
17	18	19	20	21	22	23
	TENTH COURSE SERVED					
24	25	26	27	28	29	

had been praying his entire time in the priesthood that he could win the lottery! He finally did on the most historic day ever, the Feast of Pentecost, when the entire Jewish population had to be at the Temple. A multitude of people were praying outside at the time of incense when an angel appeared to Zacharias, telling him his aged wife would conceive. This confirms our timing on the calendar.

Because of Zacharias's unbelief, he was struck silent and the angel told him he wouldn't be able to talk until his wife had given birth at the appointed time (Luke 1:20–22). As he came out of the Holy Place, he was literally speechless and was unable to close the service with the priestly blessing. Even so, he still had to stay and serve another entire week before he could go home. Imagine hearing the great news about having a child in your old age, and then having to wait a whole extra week to get started! You know his wife, Elizabeth, was now aware of all the commotion he had started, and she also had to wait a week to even see him.

The chapter goes on to say that as soon as the days of his ministration were over, he "departed"—bolted, more likely—for his own house (Luke 1:23–24). Elizabeth conceived and hid herself five months. So if she conceived the middle to the end of June, five months later puts us at the middle to the end of November. A couple of verses later we find that in her sixth month the angel Gabriel appeared to Mary (Luke 1:26–27). This is now the middle to the end of December. Guess what!

DECEMBER						
						1
2	3	4	5	6	7	8
9	10	11	12	13	14	15
16	17	18	19	20	21	22
		← HANUKAH — GABRIEL APPEARED TO MARY				
23	24	25	26	27	28	29
HANUKAH →						

This is the time of Hanukkah, the Festival of Lights, and *the* Light of the World had just been announced by an angel! Do you realize that if the Jewish revolt and the miracle commemorated by Hanukkah hadn't happened 170 years earlier, there would be no temple, no sacrifices, no priesthood, only pagan temples, pagan sacrifices, and a pagan priesthood? So the Messiah, the Light of the World, was conceived during the Festival of Lights!

The angel went on to tell Mary it was Elizabeth's sixth month, so she bolted to her cousin's house (Luke 1:39) where she remained about three more months before returning to her own home (Luke 1:56). Why? Six plus three is nine, and a pregnancy is nine months long, so she stayed to see Elizabeth's baby born, but that's not all. By now Passover had come, so she might as well stay in Jerusalem. This also puts the appointed time of the birth of Yochanan the Immerser, better known as John the Baptizer, during Passover week at the end of March or first week of April! Now, if you stop and think about it, the angel Gabriel appeared to Mary near the end of December. We know she conceived right away because of Elizabeth's response when she met up with her (Luke 1:41–45). Nine months later puts the Messiah being born around the end of September or the first of October, just in time for the Feast of Tabernacles! Here is when John would have been born:

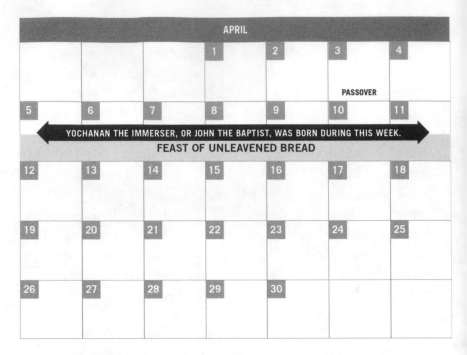

And the following calendar shows Yeshua's birth.

I am not necessarily saying He was born on September 28 or on a Sunday, but on Tishri 15, the first day of the Feast of Tabernacles, which in this particular picture appears on this date but will be pretty much a different day on our calendar every year. Let's confirm the timing a little more with our Scripture reading.

Luke 2 says that a decree had come out that everyone in the world should be registered in a census or taxed, depending on your translation (Luke 2:1). So every citizen had to travel to his or her hometown to register. Any census or registration would take at least a month or more. It wouldn't be all done in a day, especially with no planes, trains, or automobiles! Joseph, Mary's espoused husband, headed south from Nazareth to Bethlehem, which is only about three miles farther south of Jerusalem.

SEPTEMBER						
1	2	3	4	5	6	
7	8	9	10	11	12	13
14	15	16	17	18	19	20
21	22	23	24	25	26	27
28	29	30	1	2	3	4

JESUS'S WAS BORN ON TISHRI 15

FEAST OF TABERNACLES

Before we go on, I want to show you something.

Later on in this chapter we read that when Yeshua was twelve, the family went to the Passover celebrations in Jerusalem. On the way home, after a day's journey, His parents couldn't find Him. They didn't realize it earlier because they thought He was with the group of "kinfolk and acquaintances" (Luke 2:43–45). For several reasons, when Jews came to the feasts, they always traveled in groups, especially if traveling forty miles or more over several days by camel or donkey. This was not only for fellowship and security but a multitude of other reasons, such as helping with the kids. Entire towns would travel together to care for one another.

The Scriptures say Mary was great with child as she traveled to the census (2:5). She may have even been a week overdue! Do you believe the God of the Bible had all this preplanned from the beginning? Do you think He cared for Yeshua and His family? Then do you really think He would have planned for Joseph and Mary to take a forty-mile trek alone, in the middle of winter, riding on a donkey, with her being nine months pregnant, in freezing temperatures at night, where there is a high probability of heavy rains or snow during that time of year? I don't think so! No, He planned it when the weather was beautiful, and they could enjoy the trip with the entire townsfolk joining in to help during a time of great celebration. In other words, Yeshua wasn't "born on Christmas Day"!

"[When] her days were accomplished that she should be delivered . . . she brought forth her firstborn son, and wrapped him in swaddling clothes, and laid him in a manger; because there was no room at the inn" (Luke 2:6–7). Let's stop here and analyze these verses. A totally incredible detail found in the text is the wrapping in swaddling clothes. The Greek term for "'wrapping in swaddling clothes" means to wrap in strips. Remember that earlier I told you that when the priestly garments were no longer washable, being stained with the blood of the offerings, they would cut them into strips to use as wicks for the giant candelabra in the women's court of the Temple. They were stored in baskets there to be readily available. (Also remember that Mary's relative was a priest.) So what do we find but that as a newborn baby, Yeshua was wrapped in linen strips cut from the priestly garments that had been bloodstained by the sacrifices offered up on our behalf, to draw us near to God!

Why do you think there was no room at the inn? Because it was the Feast of Tabernacles, and as Josephus wrote, two and a half million people were competing for space! Most of the out-of-towners or those traveling internationally from Egypt, Syria, Jordan, and so forth, would have arrived a couple of weeks earlier to be there for the Feast of Trumpets or Yom Kippur as well, since they were traveling farther and might as well have made a vacation out of it. The men were required to stay in the sukkahs, but the women could stay anywhere. They would simply come and enjoy the sukkah during the day with all the festivities. Bethlehem was only about a forty-five-minute walk, or even less riding. The Holy Couple would have both spent the night in their sukkah, with thousands of others all camping next to them, enjoying the party and looking at the starry night sky.

Tell me something. Would you rather be in Siberia in the middle of winter, or Arizona? The hotels in Siberia are not sold out in the dead of winter, and neither would they be in Jerusalem. I have been in Jerusalem for the Feast of Tabernacles, and the hotels *are* sold out then! Common sense even dictates that "no room at the inn" puts Yeshua's birth during a feast.

The next verse says that at the time of Yeshua's birth, there were "shepherds abiding in the field, keeping watch over their flock by night." You can bet that there are no shepherds in the fields at night in the middle of winter! If you care about the sheep, you don't have them outside in the freezing rain or snow. After the Feast of Tabernacles they get penned up. November through March is the rainy season, with very heavy rains as well as snow at higher elevations. In September and October combined, you might have seven days of rain. But in December and January it's more like thirty-one days of cold rain!

When an angel appeared to the shepherds, he told them not to fear because he was bringing them tidings of great joy, to all people! The Feast of Tabernacles is known as the "Season of our Joy" when the people were commanded to rejoice for the entire week: "You shall rejoice in your feast, you, and your son, and your daughter, and your manservant, and your maidservant, and the Levite, the stranger, and the fatherless, and the widow, that are within your gates"! (Deut. 16:14). God was saying, *"I am planning the biggest and best Birthday Party in all of history for My Son, and the world will rejoice!"*

God even preplanned the "Happy Birthday" song to be sung: Psalm 118! Look at what Joseph and Mary were singing along with everyone else that gorgeous morning: "The LORD is my strength and song, and is become my salvation [Yeshua]. The voice of rejoicing and salvation [Yeshua] *is in the tabernacles* of the righteous: the right hand of the LORD does valiantly. . . . I will praise you: for you have heard me, and are become my salvation [Yeshua]" (vv. 14–16, 21; emphasis added)! Verse 24 adds, "This is the day which the LORD has made; we will rejoice and be glad in it." So the very same day they began to build the tabernacle in the wilderness, so God could tabernacle with them, and the very same day beginning the Feast of Tabernacles in Yeshua's time, the Messiah was born in the tabernacles of the righteous, and two and a half million people were unwittingly singing, "[Yeshua] is in the tabernacles of the righteous"! Only God! Luke goes on to say that "suddenly there was with the angel a multitude of the heavenly host praising God, and saying, Glory to God in the highest, and on earth peace, good will toward men" (2:13–14). It's no wonder, as they looked down from the heavenlies and saw God's magnificent handiwork! He is truly the Master Conductor of the universe, coordinating everything from the beginning. I can almost see the heavenly fireworks going off like no firework display you have ever seen!

Oh, and there's more! Do you believe God keeps His covenant? Back in Genesis, God told Abraham that the covenant between Him and Abraham, that he and all his seed must keep, was that every male had to be circumcised. The circumcision had to take place on the eighth day (Gen. 17:10–12). The Feast of Tabernacles is seven days long, and then there is the eighth day that is completely set apart. Numbers 29:35 says it was to be a solemn assembly. According to Luke, "when eight days were accomplished for the circumcising of the child," his name was called Yeshua, so named by the angel before He was conceived in the womb (Luke 2:21). Do you see what I see? If Yeshua was born on the first day of the Feast of Tabernacles, then on the eighth day He was in His Father's house, shedding His blood through the covenant of circumcision, and confirming that covenant to Abraham! Do you see all the dress rehearsals and the perfect timing of the Lord?

The timing of Yeshua's birth was so miraculous. As miraculous as the birth itself! We know from Matthew that "all this was done, that it might be fulfilled which was spoken of the Lord by the prophet, saying, Behold, a virgin shall be with child, and shall bring forth a son, and they shall call his name Emmanuel, which being interpreted is, God with us" (Matt. 1:22–23). This was a prophecy from Isaiah 7:14. Some say the Hebrew word Isaiah used for "virgin" is *almah* and means "a young woman," not necessarily a virgin; the Hebrew word *betulah* means "virgin." Actually both can mean either "virgin" or "a young maiden." *Betulah* as used in Joel 1:8 describes a young woman who is married and definitely not a virgin. And *almah* as used to describe Rebekah in Genesis 24:43 definitely means "virgin." It comes down to what the Jewish writers of the Septuagint thought it meant when they translated the Hebrew word into the Greek. Long before Yeshua was born, they chose the Greek word *parthenos*, which means "virgin." So the sages in Matthew 2 knew the Messiah would be of supernatural origins. Another proof Messiah was born at the feast of tabernacles and not Passover is that according to Luke 3:23 He began His ministry around his birthday when He was about 30 years of age. He ministered for 3½ years dying on Passover. If He was born at Passover and ministered for 3½ years He should have died during the fall feasts.

* * *

Returning to the Feast of Tabernacles, God gave us this most wonderful feast to show us what life would be like during the messianic age, when the knowledge of the Messiah will be increased and the Spirit of God will cover the earth as the waters cover the sea (Hab. 2:14). Each of the feasts has layers of fulfillment at different times. The Feast of Tabernacles began when God was tabernacling in the garden with Adam and Eve, then another layer was added when Moses' tabernacle was built. Additional layers formed when Yeshua was born, and again, when He ministered during the feast. When He returns for the thousand-year messianic reign it will find fulfillment, and again, at last, with the new heavens and the new earth.

Ironically, it is believed that the Battle of Armageddon will take place during the Feast of Tabernacles. Every year during this feast, the portion of the Bible that describes the battle of Gog and Magog, Ezekiel 38–39, is read, along with Zechariah 12–14, which prophesies that Israel's enemies will be destroyed.

What is fascinating is that God is very tactical in His warfare. Ezekiel 38 tells of a great shaking in the land of Israel that will cause the fishes of the sea, the fowls of the heavens, the beast of the fields, all creeping things, and even all the men on the face of the earth to shake at God's presence. The mountains will be thrown down, and every wall will fall to the ground (vv. 19–22).

I don't know if you have experienced an earthquake, but I have experienced a few up here in Washington State, and they are scary. Isaiah 24:19–20 tells of the earth being utterly broken down and "moved exceedingly," reeling "to and fro like a drunkard." This will take place during the Feast of Tabernacles, so I will be very glad to be in my sukkah! The word *Gog* means "roof." (Strong's number 1406.) Here we see the battle being between the house and the sukkah. A house is what man builds with a solid roof, shutting out the heavens, where you don't see God and you hope He doesn't see you. The Sukkah is a small, fragile structure with a simple top that is to be made so you can purposefully see the stars when you are looking up. So we have the strong, prideful house coming against the humility of the sukkah, in which one must rely on God. Is our security going to be found in what we can build or in the Lord?

During the Feast of Tabernacles, or Sukkot, the meals are eaten outside in the sukkah. Ezekiel 39, which, again, is read during this feast, speaks of a meal being eaten outside. The Lord tells Ezekiel to invite every feathered fowl and every beast of the field to assemble for a great sacrifice that is being prepared for them on the mountains of Israel. They will eat the flesh of the mighty and drink the blood of the princes of the earth and be filled with the flesh of the men of war and of horses (vv. 17–21). These are the very same words we find in Revelation where an angel invites all the fowls of heaven to come and join the supper of the great God (Rev. 19:17–18). I believe both Ezekiel and John were seeing the same event, and that it will unfold some year during the time of the Feast of Tabernacles.

SHABBAT

The last, but not least, divine appointment is the Sabbath, or Shabbat. It is actually the first one mentioned in Leviticus:

> And the LORD spoke unto Moses, saying, Speak to the children of Israel, and say to them, Concerning the feasts of the LORD, which you shall proclaim to be holy convocations, even these are my feasts. Six days shall work be done: but the seventh day is the sabbath of rest, an holy convocation; you shall do no work therein: it is the sabbath of the LORD in all your dwellings. (Lev. 23:1–3)

We see from the very beginning in Genesis that the first thing the Lord sanctified was the seventh day for man to rest (Gen. 2:1–2). Now, from the get-go I want to make something clear, as I know this is a hot topic. There are so many misconceptions out there it is unbelievable. I am not against going to church on Sunday, so all the swords can be put down. Temple services were held every day of the week, so they are all good days for gathering together for teaching and worship. In Lev. 6:12 we see they were required every day, even twice a day, to offer sacrifices as well as to take out the ashes, service the menorah, and so on. Daily the Levites would be leading the worship service. I personally travel all over the United States as well as internationally and teach at churches on Sunday.

But with all that said, while every day the priests were on duty, and every day of the week is a great day to have church, that doesn't make Sunday the *Sabbath*. For that matter, go to church on Sunday, but rest on the Sabbath. For many people Sunday isn't even a "Sabbath" anyway, but simply a two-hour service attended to fulfill an obligation; then the rest of the day is all about themselves.

My purpose is to show you how wonderful Shabbat is, not prove its proper timing to you theologically. And keep in mind that it is not the Jews' Sabbath; it is the Lord's Sabbath, so don't let anti-Semitism drive you away from the greatest blessing ever! Let's begin with Isaiah 56:

> For thus said the LORD to the eunuchs that keep *my* sabbaths, and choose the things that please *me*, and take hold of *my* covenant; even to them will I give in my house and within my walls a place and a name better than of sons and of daughters: I will give them an everlasting name, that shall not be cut off. Also the sons of the stranger, that join themselves to the LORD, to serve *him*, and to love the name of the LORD, to be his servants.

Now look at this wide-open comment that the Lord added:

> Everyone that keeps the sabbath from polluting it, and takes hold of *my* covenant; even them will I bring to my holy mountain, and make them joyful in my house of prayer: their burnt offerings and their sacrifices shall be accepted on my altar; for my house shall be called an house of prayer for all people. (Isa. 56:4–7; deity pronoun emphasis added)

Did you see that? God says that *everyone* who keeps the Sabbath will be brought to His holy mountain and made joyful in His house of prayer. Keeping the Sabbath is opposite of legalism. Legalism is all about works. The Sabbath is just the opposite. It's all about resting. That is the gospel! The good news is that our salvation is not based on our works, but on His work! The Sabbath is a weekly reminder of that.

The Sabbath was created before the curse came. However, work was also assigned to Adam before the curse. Therefore, both were for all mankind. However, in creating our universe, three things were required—time, space, and matter—and only one of these was declared holy in Genesis. Which one? It was *time* (Gen. 2:3 HCSB)! God sanctified a special time, setting it apart to spend with His kids, so they could build a relationship with their Creator!

The next thing God set apart was matter. According to Exodus 19:6, God sanctified a people group, telling them, "You shall be to me a kingdom of priests, and an holy nation." Later He reminded the nation of Israel that He was the One who sanctified them (Lev. 20:8).

Finally, He sanctified space (Ex. 25:8). He told Israel to make Him a sanctuary, a holy, set-apart place where He could meet with them. So first God sanctified time, His appointed time; then He sanctified His people; and finally, so they would remain sanctified, He sanctified a place, where they were to meet with Him at the appointed time.

But what did Jeroboam do, in 1 Kings? He changed the times, changed the place, and consequently changed his position with God (12:27–33). He devised in his own heart when and where He would serve God, as if he were the boss. I am not arrogant enough to think I can edit God's Word; that is too scary for me! Yeshua Himself kept the appointed Sabbath, as did the disciples after His ascension (Luke 4:16, 31; Acts 13:42–44). Did you know that when God makes the new heavens and the new earth after the millennial reign, we will *still* be keeping His weekly Sabbaths and the monthly new moon festival (Isa. 66:22, 23)? I guess He is still the same!

There is an incredible book that you can buy online called *The Sabbath* by Abraham Joshua Herschel. I've had this book forever, and I recommend any and every book that this man has ever written. I want to share with you a concept I learned from him. Let's go back to the concept of time, space, and matter.

Do you realize that most of our labor is spent in pursuit of things? We spend our *time* filling our *space* with *matter*! Then we labor harder for a bigger space to keep even more "matter"! I can't help but think of the foolish man in Luke who said, "I don't have room to store my crops, so I'll just tear these perfectly good barns down and build bigger ones" (see Luke 12:17–18)!

Most religions believe their deity resides in space, be it in rivers or in mountains or some other geographic place. We see this in 2 Kings, when the king of Assyria removed the people from the land and put them in the land of Samaria. They were being attacked by lions, and they assumed it was because they did not know the god of that land, as if each territory has its own god (2 Kings 17:26–27).

Sometimes religions associate their god with matter, like a statue. Imagine when the Greeks and Romans stormed the Temple to find the God of the Hebrews and there was nothing there! They were looking for a material God in physical space, but we know that God is a Spirit, and those who worship him must worship Him in Spirit and in truth (John 4:24). But often, because we view God as a thing made of some kind of matter, we think of His presence as residing in some space, or in nature.

The Bible is more concerned about time than about space. The God of Israel is a God of events in time. He's concerned with generations and manifests Himself in history. Thus, Judaism is a religion of time and the sanctification of it. The Bible wants us to have the same priorities. A person on his deathbed wishes he had spent his *time* differently, not acquired more stuff. To someone who is space conscious, all days are alike; there is no sanctified time. This tells you what that individual's priority is. The word *holy* means to be set apart. If everything is the same, then nothing is holy; that means everything is common.

We need to attach ourselves to holiness in time. The last thing created was the Sabbath, so that tells us it was God's goal line. Every week, as we begin our workweek, our goal is the Shabbat. We know what to do with space: we fill it. But what do we do with time as it consumes our every moment of life? We retreat to space, and again, we fill it: material becomes the great cathedral. But the Bible shows that the Sabbath is our great Cathedral. It is not about what we can build, but what God has set apart. We *build* towers of Babel. God *sets apart* appointed times, when He will intersect with human history.

Every Sabbath, including those during the feasts, was time dependent. There were specific times for the evening and morning sacrifices, and set times for prayer. We are told to remember the good times and the bad. We are to remember creation, the Passover, and the virgin birth. So the spiritual man is not concerned about the accumulation of stuff but the possibility of facing sacred moments!

Ecclesiastes 3:1 tells us that to everything there is a season and a time to every purpose under heaven. The problem is we don't know what time it is because we are not on God's calendar! We are plucking at planting time and planting at plucking time. If all time is the same, then who cares what you do or when you do it! Celebrate the Fourth of July in October. Tell your wife you're arbitrarily changing your anniversary date because it's more convenient for you in your work schedule.

We do not realize just how significant time is. Jeremiah 8:7 tells us that the stork knows her appointed time, and the turtledove, crane, and swallow all return at the right time, but God's people are clueless! (That's the MBV, or Mark Biltz Version.) In 1 Chronicles 12:32, praise was given to the sons of Issachar because they had an understanding of the times and knew what Israel ought to do. Which is more inspiring, looking at the Grand Canyon or a trench in your backyard? How about an eagle in flight compared to a mosquito on your arm? We can see the diversity in places and in matter, but we can't see the significance in the diversity in time. When we declare every day the same, we lack vision, and it is from a lack of vision that God's people perish (Prov. 29:18).

At the back of this book, I have included a simple booklet you can use to help you set the Sabbath apart. Members of our congregation, to help others find the rest and joy in keeping the Shabbat, put it together. Susie and Tony McElroy (with the help of Rachel Maxville) offer it as a separate booklet that you can get directly from them, so you don't have to carry this book around. We just wanted to share the concept with you. See the appendix.

HANUKKAH AND THE END TIMES

One of the big keys to unlocking biblical prophecy is realizing that the God of Israel tries to communicate with mankind by repeating the same events over and over from different perspectives until, hopefully, we finally figure it out. This is why Ecclesiastes 1:9 states that what has been is what shall be, and that which is done is that which will be done, for there is nothing new under the sun.

Many believers are completely unaware of the fact Yeshua kept Hanukkah, but He did. Hanukkah is a Jewish commemoration of the rededication of the Temple around 168 BCE after it was defiled and laid waste by Antiochus Epiphanes. The Maccabees overthrew the Greek armies, reestablishing the Temple service, and this is celebrated every winter on Kislev 25. The Hebrew word *Hanukkah*, alternately spelled *Chanukah*, means "dedication" in English, and it was during the Feast of Dedication in Jerusalem, in the winter, when Yeshua walked in Solomon's porch and the Jews surrounded Him, wanting to know if He was the Messiah (John 10:22–24).

Hanukkah is eight days long because eight is the number for dedication. On the eighth day, the firstfruits of everything, whether crops or animals, were to be dedicated to God (Ex. 22:29–30). Circumcision took place on the eighth day as well. It was on the eighth day in Moses' tabernacle during the dedication ceremony that the Lord appeared to Israel and fire from the Lord consumed the offerings on the altar (Lev. 9:1, 23–24). Solomon's Temple was also "chanuked," or dedicated, during the Feast of Tabernacles. It was the eighth day of the feast when the Temple was dedicated, and again fire from the Lord consumed the offerings (2 Chron. 7:8–9). King Hezekiah also chanuked the temple on the eighth day, after King Ahaz defiled it (2 Chron. 29:15–17). Around 500 BCE, when Ezra and Nehemiah returned to rebuild the Temple, they chanuked it as well (Ezra 6:3–16).

Daniel prophesied that the events surrounding Hanukkah would take place when he interpreted King Nebuchadnezzar's dream of an image with a head of gold, arms and chest of silver, belly and thighs of brass, legs of iron, and feet of iron and clay. Daniel told the king that he was the head of gold (Dan. 2:31–40). After him would come an inferior kingdom of silver, followed by two others more inferior, brass and iron, and then an end-time kingdom. So Nebuchadnezzar built the image he saw and wanted to "Chanukah" it, or dedicate it (Dan. 3:1–2). We see this pattern repeated in Revelation 13:14–15, where an image of the "beast" is made for everyone to worship.

In Daniel 7, the prophet himself had a night vision. He saw four great beasts come up from the sea. The first was like a lion, the second a bear, the third a leopard with four heads and four wings, and the fourth a dreadful beast with iron teeth and ten horns (Dan. 7:2–8). What he was seeing was the same thing that Nebuchadnezzar had dreamed, but from a different perspective.

Then Daniel foresaw the same events again, but now in yet another way. This time he saw a ram with two horns, followed by a he-goat with a "notable horn" between his eyes. This goat killed the ram and became very great. When he was strong, his great horn was broken, and in its place came four outstanding ones. Out of one of them sprouted a little horn, which also became very great, and the Bible says that "by him the daily sacrifice was taken away" (Dan. 8:3–11). Then Daniel heard two people talking, wondering how long these events—the cessation of the daily sacrifice and the trampling of the sanctuary under-foot—would continue, and was told that after 2,300 days the sanctuary would be cleansed (Dan. 8:13–14). Remember that Daniel was in Babylon at this time. The Temple was currently in ruins. So he was seeing down the road a ways.

Then the angel Gabriel gave Daniel the interpretation of his vision. He said the ram represented the Medes and Persians. Gee, this is what Nebuchadnezzar saw, from a different perspective! The goat was the king of Greece, represented by the great horn. This was speaking of Alexander the Great, whose kingdom would be broken and divided into four kingdoms, the four horns signifying their leaders. The smaller horn that rose up from one of these was referring to Antiochus Epiphanes, the Greek king in the Hanukkah story! He would become great and destroy many people through a deceitful peace process (Dan. 8:16–25).

So Nebuchadnezzar dreamed of the future kingdoms in the form of a tall image; then Daniel saw them in the form of four beasts, then again as animals. Finally, in Daniel 11, we read again about the daily sacrifice being taken away and the "abomination that makes desolate" being set up. Daniel was told that the wise would understand and would instruct many, yet even they would fall (vv. 31–33).

Nineteenth-century German philosopher Georg Hegel said that what we learn from history is that we do *not* learn from history. That's a particular problem for many prophecy buffs. Due to their Greek linear mind-set, they embrace a sort of checklist concept, where once something happens, it is "checked off," as if it can't happen again. How are they *ever* to learn from history that way?

Actually, the opposite is true. When something has happened

once, you can almost guarantee it will happen again, but in a slightly different way. Many readers applied Daniel's vision to future, end-time events when in fact they have actually already happened. But realize that that is proof that they will happen again! Let's look at actual history from 1 Maccabees:

> 1 MACCABEES 1:1: After Alexander the Macedonian, Philip's son, who came from the land of Kittim [Greece], had defeated Darius, king of the Persians and Medes, he became king in his place, having first ruled in Greece.

My goodness! This is the actual order of both Nebuchadnezzar's and Daniel's visions. Then we find further fulfillment:

> 1 MACCABEES 1:10-15: There sprang from these a sinful offshoot, Antiochus Epiphanes, son of King Antiochus, once a hostage at Rome. He became king in the one hundred and thirty-seventh year of the kingdom of the Greeks [137 BC]. In those days there appeared in Israel transgressors of the law who seduced many, saying: "Let us go and make a covenant with the Gentiles all around us; since we separated from them, many evils have come upon us." The proposal was agreeable; some from among the people promptly went to the king, and he authorized them to introduce the ordinances of the Gentiles. Thereupon they built a gymnasium in Jerusalem according to the Gentile custom. They disguised their circumcision and abandoned the holy covenant; they allied themselves with the Gentiles and sold themselves to wrongdoing.

The root meaning of the word *gym* is *naked*. The Olympics were done in the nude. This gymnasium was built right in

Jerusalem next to the Temple. The goal was to completely assimilate the Jews into Greek culture. Let's go back to history:

> 1 MACCABEES 1:20-24: After Antiochus had defeated Egypt in the one hundred and forty-third year [169 BC], he returned and went up against Israel and against Jerusalem with a strong force. He insolently entered the sanctuary [to plunder it and use its goods to pay his army] and took away the golden altar, the lampstand for the light with all its utensils, the offering table, the cups and bowls, the golden censers, and the curtain. The cornices and the golden ornament on the facade of the temple—he stripped it all off. And he took away the silver and gold and the precious vessels; he also took all the hidden treasures he could find. Taking all this, he went back to his own country. He shed much blood and *spoke with great arrogance.* [emphasis added]

Wow! This is exactly what Daniel said would happen! Now look at what happened next historically and tell me if the statement from Ecclesiastes isn't true, that what has happened before is what will happen again!

> 1 MACCABEES 1:41-50: Then the king wrote to his whole kingdom that all should be one people, and abandon their particular customs. All the Gentiles conformed to the command of the king, and many Israelites delighted in his religion; they sacrificed to idols and profaned the Sabbath. The king sent letters by messenger to Jerusalem and to the cities of Judah, ordering them to follow customs foreign to their land; to prohibit burnt offerings, sacrifices, and libations in the sanctuary, to profane the Sabbaths and feast days, to

desecrate the sanctuary and the sacred ministers, to build pagan altars and temples and shrines, to sacrifice swine and unclean animals, to leave their sons uncircumcised, and to defile themselves with every kind of impurity and abomination; so that they might forget the law and change all its ordinances. Whoever refused to act according to the command of the king was to be put to death.

This is incredible! We are seeing shades of these events right now in our own lifetime. So then what happens:

1 MACCABEES 1:54-57: On the fifteenth day of the month Kislev, in the year one hundred and forty-five [December 7, 167 BC], the king erected the desolating abomination upon the altar of burnt offerings, and in the surrounding cities of Judah they built pagan altars. They also burned incense at the doors of houses and in the streets. Any scrolls of the law [books of the Pentateuch] that they found they tore up and burned. Whoever was found with a scroll of the covenant, and whoever observed the law, was condemned to death by royal decree.

Can you imagine it? This is the abomination of desolation spoken of by Daniel the prophet, appearing almost two hundred years before the Messiah's birth. So now comes the story of the Judean rebellion!

1 MACCABEES 1:62-64; 2:15-28: But many in Israel were determined and resolved in their hearts not to eat anything unclean; they preferred to die rather than to be defiled with food or to profane the holy covenant; and they did die. And very great wrath came upon Israel. . . . The officers of the

king in charge of enforcing the apostasy came to the city of Modein to make them sacrifice. Many of Israel joined them, but Mattathias and his sons drew together. Then the officers of the king addressed Mattathias: "You are a leader, an honorable and great man in this city, supported by sons and kindred. Come now, be the first to obey the king's command, as all the Gentiles and Judeans and those who are left in Jerusalem have done. Then you and your sons shall be numbered among the King's Friends, and you and your sons shall be honored with silver and gold and many gifts." But Mattathias answered in a loud voice: "Although all the Gentiles in the king's realm obey him, so that they forsake the religion of their ancestors and consent to the king's orders, yet I and my sons and my kindred will keep to the covenant of our ancestors. Heaven forbid that we should forsake the law and the commandments. We will not obey the words of the king by departing from our religion in the slightest degree." As he finished saying these words, a certain Jew came forward in the sight of all to offer sacrifice on the altar in Modein according to the king's order. When Mattathias saw him, he was filled with zeal; his heart was moved and his just fury was aroused; he sprang forward and killed him upon the altar. At the same time, he also killed the messenger of the king who was forcing them to sacrifice, and he tore down the altar. Thus he showed his zeal for the law, just as Phinehas did with Zimri, son of Salu. Then Mattathias cried out in the city, "Let everyone who is zealous for the law and who stands by the covenant follow me!" Then he and his sons fled to the mountains, leaving behind in the city all their possessions.

Pay close attention also to what unfolded next:

1 MACCABEES 2:32-41: Many hurried out after them, and having caught up with them, camped opposite and *prepared to attack them on the sabbath.* The pursuers said to them, "Enough of this! Come out and obey the king's command, and you will live." But they replied, "We will not come out, nor will we obey the king's command to profane the sabbath." Then the enemy attacked them at once. *But they did not retaliate;* they neither threw stones, nor blocked up their secret refuges. They said, "Let us all die in innocence; heaven and earth are our witnesses that you destroy us unjustly." So the officers and soldiers attacked them on the sabbath, and they died with their wives, their children and their animals, to the number of a thousand persons. When Mattathias and his friends heard of it, they mourned deeply for them. They said to one another, "If we all do as our kindred have done, and do not fight against the Gentiles for our lives and our laws, they will soon destroy us from the earth." *So on that day they came to this decision: "Let us fight against anyone who attacks us on the sabbath, so that we may not all die as our kindred died in their secret refuges."* [emphasis added]

This was a historic decision that winter, as it was determined after they fled to the mountains, that they could defend themselves on the Sabbath. Now let's go to Josephus, who lived during the first century, and read what he wrote concerning these epic events:

JOSEPHUS, ANTIQUITIES OF THE JEWS, BOOK 12, CHAPTERS 6-7: When therefore the generals of Antiochus's

armies had been beaten so often, Judas assembled the people
together, and told them, that after these many victories which
God had given them, they ought to go up to Jerusalem, and
purify the temple, and offer the appointed sacrifices. But as
soon as he, with the whole multitude, was come to Jerusalem,
and found the temple deserted, and its gates burnt down, and
plants growing in the temple of their own accord, on account
of its desertion, he and those that were with him began
to lament, and were quite confounded at the sight of the
temple; so he chose out some of his soldiers, and gave them
order to fight against those guards that were in the citadel,
until he should have purified the temple. When therefore
he had carefully purged it, and had brought in new vessels,
the candlestick, the table [of shew-bread], and the altar [of
incense], which were made of gold, he hung up the veils at
the gates, and added doors to them. He also took down the
altar [of burnt-offering], and built a new one of stones that
he gathered together, and not of such as were hewn with
iron tools. So on the five and twentieth day of the month
Casleu, which the Macedonians call Apeliens, they lighted
the lamps that were on the candlestick, and offered incense
upon the altar [of incense], and laid the loaves upon the
table [of shew-bread], and offered burnt-offerings upon the
new altar [of burnt-offering]. Now it so fell out, that these
things were done on the very same day on which their divine
worship had fallen off, and was reduced to a profane and
common use, after three years' time; for so it was, that the
temple was made desolate by Antiochus, and so continued
for three years. . . . *And this desolation came to pass according
to the prophecy of Daniel, which was given four hundred and*

eight years before; for he declared that the Macedonians would dissolve that worship [for some time].

7. Now Judas celebrated the festival of the restoration of the sacrifices of the temple for *eight days*, and omitted no sort of pleasures thereon; but he feasted them upon very rich and splendid sacrifices; and he honoured God, and delighted them by hymns and psalms. Nay, they were so very glad at the revival of their customs, when, after a long time of intermission, they unexpectedly had regained the freedom of their worship, that they made it a law for their posterity, that they should keep a festival, on account of the restoration of their temple worship, for eight days. And from that time to this we celebrate this festival, and call it Lights. [emphasis added]

So we see that the people who lived during the time of Yeshua considered the prophecy in Daniel to be already fulfilled 200 years earlier during Hanukkah.

Now we go to the time of Messiah in the first century and reread Matthew 24, concerning what will happen in the end times. We find Yeshua sitting on the Mount of Olives:

And Jesus said to them, See you not all these things? truly I say to you, There shall not be left here one stone on another, that shall not be thrown down. And as he sat on the mount of Olives, the disciples came to him privately, saying, Tell us, when shall these things be? and what shall be the sign of your coming, and of the end of the world? And Jesus answered and said to them. . . . They [shall] deliver you up to be afflicted, and shall kill you: and you shall be hated of all nations for my name's sake. 10 And then shall many be offended, and shall betray one another, and shall hate one another. 11 And many false prophets shall rise, and shall deceive many. 12 And because iniquity shall abound, the love of many shall wax cold. (Matt. 24:2–4, 9–12).

In their minds the disciples were seeing the events of Hanukkah happening all over again, because that is literally and historically what happened, as the Hellenistic-minded Jews wanted nothing to do with the religious Jews. They hated and fought among themselves. Yeshua continued:

> When you therefore shall see the abomination of desolation, spoken of by Daniel the prophet, stand in the holy place, (whoever reads, let him understand:) Then let them which be in Judaea flee into the mountains: Let him which is on the housetop not come down to take any thing out of his house: Neither let him which is in the field return back to take his clothes. (Matt. 24:15–18)

Good heavens! the disciples must have thought. *This is exactly what happened two hundred years ago—and now it's going to happen again!*

To cap it off, Yeshua told them to pray that their flight would not be in the winter, or on the Sabbath day (Matt. 24:20–21). Remember that Hanukkah was instituted in the winter, and the Sabbath was when the Jews of that day refused to put up a fight and died at the hands of Antiochus's forces. Can you see why the disciples felt He was saying that the events leading to Hanukkah would happen again? Unless believers understand the history of Hanukkah, they won't have a clear understanding of end times!

I like to ask people if they can see the differences between Hanukkah with Antiochus Epiphanes, and Purim with Haman in the book of Esther. Haman wanted complete annihilation of the Jewish people, regardless of their compliance with the current government. *Just kill them all*, was his plan. Haman represented satan for sure. Antiochus, though, wasn't about annihilation as much as he was about assimilation. Sure, he would kill those who wouldn't assimilate, but assimilation, not extermination, was the goal. I believe the Antichrist will not be like Haman as much as he will be like Antiochus. This is why so many will be deceived. The unbelievers are already deceived. What we see happening right now is the assimilation of believers as they fall for Chrislam believing that allah and the God of the Bible are the same. Islam's allah has no son, so how in the world could someone who believes in Yeshua think they are the same? What I see unfolding is a situation in which believers will be told that they can keep their Jesus; they just also have to bow down to the image. The church has been so compromised and deceived already with the teachings of cheap grace, or hyper-grace, which maintains that all their sins—past, present, and future—are forgiven, so they can sin all they want. They will have no problem bowing to an idol, as they can just pull out their Jesus from their pockets when they need Him. After all, all that Old Testament law stuff is completely done away with! Really? I'd like to offer them a passage from the New Testament that might change their point of view:

> For the mystery of iniquity does already work: only he who now lets will let, until he be taken out of the way. And then shall that Wicked [One] be revealed, whom the Lord shall

consume with the spirit of his mouth, and shall destroy with the brightness of his coming: Even him, whose coming is after the working of Satan with all power and signs and lying wonders. (2 Thess. 2:7–9)

Do you realize that the word *Wicked* used here comes from the Greek word *anomos*, meaning "destitute of law" or "lawless"? So the Wicked One is also the lawless one. What law was Paul talking about? He wasn't talking about the laws of the United Nations or of Iran or Las Vegas! The Antichrist opposes Torah, the Mosaic law, God's instructions on how to live and treat people. The passage goes on to say that this lawless one will deceive those who do not have a love for the truth. Therefore, God will send them a "strong delusion, that they should believe a lie"—and be damned (vv. 9–12).

BLOOD MOONS: DECODING THE IMMINENT HEAVENLY SIGNS

Many have asked me, "What now, since the blood moons have passed?" They are referring to my book *Blood Moons*, in which I linked the feast days in the Bible with the lunar eclipses of 2014 and 2015, as well as other years throughout history. People say my theory was all wrong. My only comment is, what planet do they live on? First, it wasn't a "theory." That eclipses occur is a fact, not a theory. It is also a fact that these particular eclipses occurred on the biblical feast days. NASA does not have theories when eclipses occur, but raw data. I do not control an eclipse. Neither do I control the biblical calendar. The Bible clearly says that God created the sun and the moon for signs (Gen. 1:14). I did not write the Bible. And it is a fact, not a theory, that major, biblically significant historical events have occurred during or around the time that eclipses occurred on the feast days. I did not write history either.

With that said, what I did say, based on these facts, was that there was a high probability that if the historical patterns stayed true, we could also see a couple of critical things happen surrounding the years 2014 and 2015. I was never date-specific, as some others were. What I said could possibly happen was a war with Israel, which, in fact, did happen between the blood moons of April and October in 2014. I still believe another, larger Middle East war could unfold. I also said there was a good possibility the economy could collapse, especially in 2016. As I am currently about to publish this book, in April 2016, I can't help but say to all the naysayers, "I told you so!"

To those who have not read my other book, I highly recommend you read it right away, as it is still relevant and always will be. I give the scientific, historical, and biblical proof that God uses the sun and the moon as signs to warn humankind of coming events! When a bridge is out on a major highway, the highway department doesn't put the warning sign right where the bridge is out, but at least a mile ahead, if not much more. The warning signs we received from the heavens in 2014 and 2015, I believe, were for more than just those years but also for 2016 and beyond.

Look at what transpired back then with the rise of ISIS, the Ebola outbreak, the war in Gaza, to name but a few. Since the blood moons of 2014–15, we have seen a rise of blood in the streets from Paris to San Bernardino, California, to more than three thousand terror attacks on the streets of Israel. We have seen the collapse of the economy starting in January of this year. We see the rise of the possibility of a major war in the Middle

East as Saudi Arabia and Iran go at it. What's next?

I do hope that after reading this book, along with the companion book, *Blood Moons: Decoding the Imminent Heavenly Signs*, you can see the importance of being on God's calendar and celebrating His divine appointments so you can walk hand in hand with the God of Abraham, Isaac, and Israel. We don't want to get ahead or behind, but as Noah, Enoch, Abraham, and many others have walked with Him, may you also walk side by side with the Mighty One of Israel!

APPENDIX 1

THE PASSOVER SEDER FOR BELIEVERS IN YESHUA

This day shall be to you for a memorial, and you shall keep it a feast to the LORD: throughout your generations you shall keep it a feast by an ordinance forever.

Exodus 12:14 (HNV)

He took bread, and when he had given thanks, he broke it, and gave to them, saying, "This is my body which is given for you. Do this in memory of me."

Luke 22:19 (HNV)

INTRODUCTION

It's exciting to be here at this appointed time. Passover is not something we just decided to do; it is something the Creator of the universe has asked us to do! Don't you think we should honor His request?

During Passover, you are going to be part of history. We

are going to be forging one more link in a chain that goes back for 3,500 years. The word *Seder* means "order." For over 2,000 years there has been a specific order to the story of redemption. Through our Passover Seder, we are going to tell the story of redemption in a most dramatic way. We will travel from the original Passover, in Egypt, to Messiah's Passover, which was known as the Last Supper, to our Passover right now.

We are going to see all three of these Passovers merge together as we see God's hand move upon us as we keep the feast.

As we read the Scriptures, you will see that we use two different versions of the Bible in this Haggadah. They are the Hebrew Names Version (HNV) and the English Standard Version (ESV).

KADESH: BENEDICTION/SANCTIFYING

We start by setting the time apart with prayer.

Each of us is to regard ourselves as though we were personally being redeemed out of Egypt from Egyptian slavery. Regard it tonight as if you have just escaped Egypt yourself.

Lighting the Festival Candles

All stand for the lighting and blessings as the woman of the house lights the menorah from left to right.

Woman:

Ba-ruch At-ah Adonai E-Lo-hei-nu Me-lech Ha-olam, A-sher Kid-sha-nu B'mitz-vo-tav v'tzi-va-nu Le-had-lik Ner Shel Yom Tov.

All Together:

Blessed are You, O Lord our God, King of the universe, who has set us apart by Your Word and in whose name we light the festival lights.

Shehecheyanu: "He Supports Us"
We say this prayer to set the time apart.

All Together:

Ba-ruch At-ah Adonai E-lo-hei-nu Me-lech Ha-olam, She-he-che-yanu Ve-kee-ya-manu ve-hi-gee-ya-nu Laz-aman ha-zeh.

All Together:

Blessed are You, Lord our God, King of the universe, who has supported us, protected us, and brought us to this season.

From the Amidah: "The Standing Prayer"
This prayer is 2,400 years old and is said three times a day. This is the prayer the disciples were saying in the Upper Room when Yeshua appeared to them.

All Together:

You, O Lord, are mighty forever. You revive the dead. You have the power to save. You sustain the living with loving-kindness; You revive the dead with great mercy. You support the falling, heal the sick, set free the bound, and keep faith with those who sleep in the dust. Who is like You, O Doer of mighty acts? Who resembles You, a King who puts to death, and restores to life, and causes salvation to flourish?

And You are certain to revive the dead. Blessed are You, O Lord, who revives the dead. Just as God commanded the light to shine at creation, let us ask Yeshua to bring light into the dark areas of our life.

All Together:

2 Corinthians 4:5–6 (HNV): For we don't preach ourselves, but Messiah Yeshua as Lord, and ourselves as your servants for Yeshua's sake; seeing it is God who said, "Light will shine out of darkness," who shined in our hearts, to give the light of the knowledge of the glory of God in the face of Yeshua the Messiah.

Blowing of the Shofar

At Mount Sinai when a resounding shofar was heard, the shofar was speaking of God's voice. We blow the shofar so we learn to listen for God's voice.

Exodus 19:16–19 (HNV): It happened on the third day, when it was morning, that there were thunders and lightning, and a thick cloud on the mountain, and the sound of an exceedingly loud shofar; and all the people who were in the camp trembled. Moshe led the people out of the camp to meet God; and they stood at the lower part of the mountain. Mount Sinai, the whole of it, smoked, because the LORD descended on it in fire; and its smoke ascended like the smoke of a furnace, and the whole mountain quaked greatly. When the sound of the shofar grew louder and louder, Moshe spoke, and God answered him by a voice.

(All may be seated.)

SEDER: "ORDER" (I.E., ORDER OF SERVICE)

KADESH	Benediction—sanctifying and setting the time apart / drink from the first cup
URCHATZ	Purification, where we symbolically wash our hands
KARPAS	Dipping parsley into salt water and eating it
YACHATZ	Breaking the matzah the middle one is broken and part of it is hidden
MAGGID	The Haggadah, or telling of the story of redemption and the four questions
RACHTZAH	Washing of hands before the meal / drink from the second cup
MOTSI	Customary blessing before the breaking of bread
MATZAH	Blessing for the bread
MAROR	Blessing over bitter herbs
KORECH	Make a sandwich of Matzah, bitter herbs, and charoset
SHULCHAN ORECH	Eat the Passover meal
TZAFN	Out of hiding, the Matzah that was hidden is found and eaten / drink from the third cup
BARECH	Blessing after the meal
HALLEL	Songs of praise, reading of the selected psalms

NITZAH   Acceptance, drink from the fourth cup / drink from the fifth cup if desired

THE STORY OF PASSOVER HAS TWO BEGINNINGS

1. Spiritual: Our first steps were into spiritual slavery.

> **Joshua 24:2 (ESV):** And Joshua said to all the people, "Thus says the LORD, the God of Israel, 'Long ago, your fathers lived beyond the Euphrates, Terah, the father of Abraham and of Nahor; and they served other gods.

2. Physical: Brotherly hatred led them into physical slavery.

> **Genesis 37:28 (ESV):** Midianite traders passed by. And they drew Joseph up and lifted him out of the pit, and sold him to the Ishmaelites for twenty shekels of silver. They took Joseph to Egypt.

Why we need to observe the Passover Seder

> **1 Corinthians 10:11 (ESV):** Now these things happened to them as an example, but they were written down for our instruction, on whom the end of the ages has come.

THE FOUR TYPES OF CHILDREN

Innocent Child

> **Exodus 13:8–9 (ESV):** "You shall tell your son on that day, 'It is because of what the LORD did for me when I came out of Egypt.'"

> *For the innocent child, the Bible is a closed book waiting for someone to open it and explain the relevance of redemption.*

Simple Child

Exodus 13:14 (ESV): "And when in time to come your son asks you, 'What does this mean?' you shall say to him, 'By a strong hand the LORD brought us out of Egypt, from the house of slavery.'"

For the simple child, the Word of God is an open book, since he asks questions and is looking for answers.

Wise Child

Deuteronomy 6:20–21 (ESV): "When your son asks you in time to come, 'What is the meaning of the testimonies and the statutes and the rules that the LORD our God has commanded you?' then you shall say to your son, 'We were Pharaoh's slaves in Egypt. And the LORD brought us out of Egypt with a mighty hand.'"

For the wise child, he is always looking for deeper meaning. The Torah is to be read and studied.

Wicked Child

Exodus 12:26–27 (ESV): "And when your children say to you, 'What do you mean by this service?' you shall say, 'It is the sacrifice of the LORD's Passover, for he passed over the houses of the people of Israel in Egypt, when he struck the Egyptians but spared our houses.'" And the people bowed their heads and worshiped.

For the wicked child, the Passover traditions burn up as the relevance of the Torah is destroyed.

THE FOUR CUPS

There are four stages to our redemption that are represented by the four cups, based on the following verse:

Exodus 6:6–7 (HNV): "Therefore tell the children of Yisra'el, 'I am the LORD, and I will bring you out from under the burdens of the Mitzrim [Egyptians], and I will rid you out of their bondage, and I will redeem you with an outstretched arm, and with great judgments: and I will take you to me for a people, and I will be to you a God.

(1) Sanctification

(2) Deliverance

(3) Redemption

(4) Acceptance

EXPLAINING THE FOUR CUPS

- The Lord has chosen you. You have been set apart. He has lifted your burdens.

- Your burdens have been lifted, but you are still in bondage. The Lord has now broken your chains.

- Your burdens have been lifted and the chains have been broken, but you are still in Egypt. The price has been paid; you are free to go!

- The Lord takes you as his people. You enter a relationship with the Lord, and He will be your God.

Luke 22:17 (ESV): And he took a cup, and when he had given thanks he said, "Take this, and divide it among yourselves."

FIRST CUP: KIDDUSH: THE CUP OF SANCTIFICATION
Our first step is to separate ourselves.

All stand while the leader/father fills the cups with grape juice or wine.

All Together:

Ba-ruch At-ah Adonai E-lo-hei-nu Me-lech Ha-olam,

Bo-rey Pri Ha-ga-fen. Amen.

All together:

Blessed are You, Lord our God, King of the universe, who

creates the fruit of the vine. Amen.

(All drink.)

All together:

Yeshua, free me from the yoke of this world, with all of its burdens and cares.

PRAY FOR THE NATION OF ISRAEL
Leader/Father:

Psalm 122:6–8 (ESV): Pray for the peace of Jerusalem! "May they be secure who love you! Peace be within your walls and security within your towers!" For my brothers and companions' sake I will say, "Peace be within you.

(All may be seated except leader/father.)

URCHATZ: PURIFICATION

Leader may stand in for the group, and washes his/her hands by pouring water over them and drying them.

> **Psalm 24:3–4 (ESV):** Who shall ascend the hill of the LORD? And who shall stand in his holy place? He who has clean hands and a pure heart, who does not lift up his soul to what is false and does not swear deceitfully.

KARPAS: PARSLEY

The parsley, which represents the hyssop on the doorpost, is dipped in salt water representing the tears shed in Egyptian slavery.

> *All stand for the blessing and dip a sprig of parsley into the salt water.*

> *All Together:*

> Ba-ruch At-ah Adonai E-lo-hei-nu Me-lech Ha-olam, Bo-rey Pri Ha-adamah.

> *All Together:*

> Blessed are You, Lord our God, King of the universe, who creates the fruit of the earth. Amen.

> Eat the parsley dipped in salt water.

> *(All may be seated.)*

THE FEASTS OF THE LORD

Leviticus 23:2 (ESV): "Speak to the people of Israel and say to them, These are the appointed feasts of the LORD that you shall proclaim as holy convocations; they are my appointed feasts."

Feasts mean appointments! And they are dress rehearsals!

Leviticus 23:4–7 (ESV): "These are the appointed feasts of the LORD, the holy convocations, which you shall proclaim at the time appointed for them. In the first month, on the fourteenth day of the month at twilight, is the LORD's Passover. And on the fifteenth day of the same month is the Feast of Unleavened Bread to the LORD; for seven days you shall eat unleavened bread. On the first day you shall have a holy convocation; you shall not do any ordinary work."

Bedikat Chametz: Cleaning out Leaven—Spring Cleaning

Exodus 13:7–10 (HNV): "Unleavened bread shall be eaten throughout the seven days; and no leavened bread shall be seen with you, neither shall there be yeast seen with you, in all your borders. You shall tell your son in that day, saying, 'It is because of that which the LORD did for me when I came out of Mitzrayim [Egypt].' It shall be for a sign to you on your hand, and for a memorial between your eyes, that the law of the LORD may be in your mouth; for with a strong hand the LORD has brought you out of Mitzrayim [Egypt]. You shall therefore keep this ordinance in its season from year to year."

We have a family go through the symbolic act of removing leaven by searching for a breadcrumb with a wooden spoon, feather, candle, and linen cloth.

The Candle: God's Word

Psalm 119:105 (HNV): Your word is a lamp to my feet, and a light for my path.

The Feather: The Holy Spirit

Psalm 91:4 (HNV): He will cover you with His [feathers]. Under His wings you will take refuge.

The Wooden Spoon: The Cross

Deuteronomy 21:22 (HNV): If a man have committed a sin worthy of death, and he be put to death, and you hang him on a tree . . .

Leaven: Sin/Wrong Teaching

Matthew 16:6 (ESV): Jesus said to them, "Watch and beware of the leaven of the Pharisees and Sadducees."

The Linen Cloth: Messiah's Burial Cloth

Mark 15:46 (HNV): He bought a linen cloth, and taking him down, wound him in the linen cloth, and laid him in a tomb which had been cut out of a rock.

Taken Outside/Burned: Sacrificed outside the Camp

Hebrews 13:13 (HNV): Let us therefore go forth to him outside of the camp, bearing his reproach.

BLESSING: REMOVAL OF LEAVEN

All Together:

Ba-ruch At-ah Adonai E-lo-hei-nu Me-lech Ha-olam, A-sher Kid-sha-nu B'mitz-vo-tav v'tzi-va-nu Al Buir Cha-metz.

All Together:

Blessed are You, Lord our God, King of the universe, who has sanctified us with His commandments and commands us concerning the elimination of leaven.

A reminder that Yeshua helped His Father remove leaven from Their house:

> **John 2:13–16 (HNV):** The Pesach [Passover] of the Yehudim [in Judea] was at hand, and Yeshua went up to Yerushalayim [Jerusalem]. He found in the temple those who sold oxen, sheep, and doves, and the changers of money sitting. He made a whip of cords, and threw all out of the temple, both the sheep and the oxen; and he poured out the changers' money, and overthrew their tables. To those who sold the doves, he said, "Take these things out of here! Don't make my Father's house a marketplace!"

We need to remove the spiritual leaven out of our physical house as well.

> **Hebrews 3:5–9 (HNV):** [Moses] indeed was faithful in all his house as a servant, for a testimony of those things which were

afterward to be spoken, but Messiah is faithful as a Son over his house; whose house we are, if we hold fast our confidence and the glorying of our hope firm to the end. Therefore, even as the Ruach HaKodesh [Holy Spirit] says, "Today if you will hear his voice, don't harden your hearts, as in the provocation, like as in the day of the trial in the wilderness, where your fathers tested me by proving me, and saw my works for forty years."

REMOVING SPIRITUAL LEAVEN

1 Corinthians 5:6–8 (HNV): Your boasting is not good. Don't you know that a little yeast leavens the whole lump? Purge out the old yeast, that you may be a new lump, even as you are unleavened. For indeed Messiah, our Pesach [Passover], has been sacrificed in our place. Therefore let us keep the feast, not with old yeast, neither with the yeast of malice and wickedness, but with the matzah [unleavened bread] of sincerity and truth.

Psalm 139:23–24 (HNV): Search me, God, and know my heart. Try me, and know my thoughts. See if there is any wicked way in me, and lead me in the everlasting way.

YACHATZ: BREAKING THE AFIKOMEN
Leader/Father:
Break the middle matzah in two pieces, one larger than the other. Return the smaller portion while placing the larger portion in the afikomen bag/napkin.

Put the afikomen on the shoulder and say: "In haste did we go out of Egypt!"
Hide the afikomen from the kids.

> **Exodus 12:34** (HNV): The people took their dough before it was leavened, their kneading-troughs being bound up in their clothes on their shoulders.

> **Luke 22:19** (HNV): He took bread, and when he had given thanks, he broke it, and gave to them, saying, "This is my body which is given for you. Do this in memory of me."

Leader/Father:
Show how the matzah is striped, pierced, and burnt. Tell how Yeshua was without sin and was wrapped in linen and hidden away.

MAGGID: TELLING OF THE PASSOVER STORY

> **Exodus 4:22–23** (HNV): "You shall tell [Pharaoh], 'Thus says the LORD, [Israel] is my son, my firstborn, and I have said to you, "Let my son go, that he may serve me"; and you have refused to let him go. Behold, I will kill your son, your firstborn.'"

The Four Questions
To be asked by four children:

1. Why on all other nights do we eat leavened or unleavened but on this night only unleavened bread?

2. Why on all other nights do we eat all kinds of herbs but on this night only bitter?

3. Why on all other nights do we never dip matzah but on this night we do?

4. Why on all other nights do we eat sitting, but on this night we recline?

John 13:23–26 (HNV): One of his disciples, whom Yeshua loved, was at the table, leaning against Yeshua's breast. [Simon Peter] therefore beckoned to him, and said to him, "Tell us who it is of whom he speaks." He, leaning back, as he was, on Yeshua's breast, asked him, "Lord, who is it?" Yeshua therefore answered, "It is he to whom I will give this piece of bread when I have dipped it." So when he had dipped the piece of bread, he gave it to [Judas], the son of [Simon Iscariot].

Answering the Four Questions:

This night is different because it is on this night we are told to pass on the Passover story as recorded in the book of Exodus. If God hadn't redeemed our ancestors from slavery to Egypt, we would still be slaves today. We now show appreciation to God for delivering us! We eat bitter herbs to remind us of the bitter slavery with which we served the Egyptians and the sweetness we now have of serving God. We dip the matzah in the bitter herbs and eat to remind us we need to internalize the truths of the Passover today. We recline because now we are free and slaves had to stand to eat.

Rehearsing of the Ten Plagues

Exodus 12:12 (HNV): "For I will go through the land of [Egypt] in that night, and will strike all the firstborn in the land of [Egypt], both man and animal. Against all the gods of [Egypt] I will execute judgments: I am the LORD.

Egyptian Gods versus the Plagues
Hapi, god of the Nile

- The annual flooding of the Nile was believed to be the arrival of Hapi.

- The Nile turned to blood, representing the death of Hapi.

Heqet, frog goddess of fertility

- Because the Egyptians saw that there were many frogs, all appearing from the Nile, they associated the frog with fertility and resurrection.

- God overran Egypt with frogs.

Geb, god of the earth

- Earthquakes were believed to be the laughter of Geb.

- God turned the dust into lice.

Shu, god of dry air, winds, and the atmosphere

- Shu was believed to hold the sky off the earth, allowing life to flourish with his breath.

- God brought swarms of insects.

Apis, a bull believed to be god incarnate

- The bull symbolized the king's courageous heart, great strength, virility, and fighting spirit.

- God brought death to the livestock.

Heka, god of magic and medicine

- To the Egyptians, magic and medicine were the same. Heka was a man carrying a magic staff and a knife, the tools of a healer.

- God brought boils to the people.

Nut, god of the firmament

- Nut was believed to protect man from the heavens.

- God brought hailstones.

Min, god of the harvest/vegetation

- The Egyptians celebrated the spring harvest with a festival dedicated to Min, who protected the crops.

- God brought locusts to destroy the crops.

Ra, Egyptian sun god

- Ra was believed to have brought life.

- God brought darkness.

Amon-Ra, the lamb god

- Amon-Ra was believed to have been the creator of man.

- God brought death to the firstborn of man.

RECITING THE TEN PLAGUES

The juice is a representation of the blood and death of the Egyptian gods. Everyone at the table should dip a finger in the juice and touch it to the napkin at the mention of each plague.

All Together:

- Blood

- Frogs

- Lice

- Swarms (Insects)

- Cattle plague

- Boils

- Hail

- Locusts

- Darkness

- Death of firstborn

Numbers 33:3–4 (HNV): They journeyed from Ra'meses in the first month, on the fifteenth day of the first month; on the next day after the [Passover] the children of [Israel] went out with a high hand in the sight of all the [Egyptians], while the [Egyptians] were burying all their firstborn, whom the LORD had struck among them: on their gods also the LORD executed judgments.

DAYENU! IT WOULD HAVE BEEN ENOUGH

Dayenu, a traditional song sung during Passover, is used to show our gratefulness and appreciation to God for redeeming us. We thank Him by saying: "Dayenu: Enough!"

> Had He brought us out from Egypt
> and not executed judgment against them,
> It would have been enough! Dayenu!

> Had He executed judgment against them
> and not destroyed their idols,
> It would been enough! Dayenu!

> Had He destroyed their idols
> and not slain their firstborn,
> It would been enough! Dayenu!

> Had He slain their firstborn
> and not given us their possessions,
> It would have been enough! Dayenu!

> Had He given us their possessions
> and not divided the sea for us,
> It would have been enough! Dayenu!

> Had He divided the sea for us
> and not brought us through it dry-shod,

It would have been enough! Dayenu!

Had He brought us through it dry-shod
and not drowned our oppressors in it,
It would have been enough! Dayenu!

Had He drowned our oppressors in it
and not sustained us in the wilderness for forty years,
It would have been enough! Dayenu!

Had He sustained us in the wilderness for forty years
and not fed us manna,
It would have been enough Dayenu!

Had He fed us manna
and not given us the Sabbath,
It would have been enough! Dayenu!

Had He given us the Sabbath
and not brought us to Mount Sinai,
It would have been enough! Dayenu!

Had he brought us to Mount Sinai,
and not given us the Torah,
It would have been enough! Dayenu!

Had he given us the Torah
and not brought us in the land of Israel,
It would have been enough! Dayenu!

Had He brought us into the Land of Israel
and not built the temple for us,
It would have been enough! Dayenu!

THE SEDER TRAY: EXPLAINING THE ELEMENTS

Shank bone:
Represents the lamb slain on our behalf.

Bitter herbs:
Represent the bitterness of the bondage.

Charoset:
Represents the sweetness of our deliverance.

Roasted egg:
Represents the destruction of the Temple twice on the same day.

Parsley:
Represents the hyssop dipped in the basin of blood.

Now we tell the story of how Yeshua delivered us by connecting both redemption stories:

John 12:1–2 (HNV): Six days before the [Passover], Yeshua came to [Bethany], where [Lazarus] was, who had been dead, whom he raised from the dead. So they made him a supper there. [Martha] served, but [Lazarus] was one of those who sat at the table with him.

This was the eighth of Nisan.

John 12:12–15 (HNV): On the next day a great multitude had come to the feast. When they heard that Yeshua was coming to [Jerusalem], they took the branches of the palm trees, and went out to meet him, and cried out, "Hoshia'na! Blessed is he who comes in the name of the Lord, the King

of [Israel]!" Yeshua, having found a young donkey, sat on it. As it is written, "Don't be afraid, daughter of [Zion]. Behold, your King comes, sitting on a donkey's colt."
This was the ninth, going into the tenth of Nisan.

Exodus 12:3–6 (ESV): Tell all the congregation of Israel that on the tenth day of this month every man shall take a lamb according to their fathers' houses, a lamb for a household. And if the household is too small for a lamb, then he and his nearest neighbor shall take according to the number of persons; according to what each can eat you shall make your count for the lamb. Your lamb shall be without blemish, a male a year old. You may take it from the sheep or from the goats, and you shall keep it until the fourteenth day of this month, when the whole assembly of the congregation of Israel shall kill their lambs at twilight.

Luke 13:34–35 (HNV): "[Jerusalem, Jerusalem], that kills the prophets, and stones those who are sent to her! How often I wanted to gather your children together, like a hen gathers her own brood under her wings, and you refused! Behold, your house is left to you desolate. I tell you, you will not see me, until you say, 'Blessed is he who comes in the name of the Lord!'"

Inspection of the Lamb

Matthew 26:59–61 (HNV): Now the [chief priests], the [elders], and the whole council sought false testimony against Yeshua, that they might put him to death; and they found none. Even though many false witnesses came forward, they found none. But at last two false witnesses came forward, and said, "This man said, 'I am able to destroy the temple of God, and to build it in three days.'"

Luke 23:13–15 (HNV): Pilate called together the chief [priests] and the rulers and the people, and said to them, "You brought this man to me as one that perverts the people, and see, I have examined him before you, and found no basis for a charge against this man concerning those things of which you accuse him. Neither has Herod, for I sent you to him, and see, nothing worthy of death has been done by him."

Exodus 12:7–11 (HNV): They shall take some of the blood, and put it on the two side-posts and on the lintel, on the houses in which they shall eat it. They shall eat the flesh in that night, roasted with fire, and [unleavened bread]. They shall eat it with bitter herbs. Don't eat it raw, nor boiled at all with water, but roasted with fire; with its head, its legs and its inner parts. You shall let nothing of it remain until the morning; but that which remains of it until the morning you shall burn with fire. This is how you shall eat it: with your belt on your waist, your shoes on your feet, and your staff in your hand; and you shall eat it in haste: it is the LORD's [Passover].

SECOND CUP: THE CUP OF DELIVERANCE
Stand for blessing:

All together:

Ba-ruch At-ah Adonai E-lo-hei-nu Me-lech Ha-olam,

Bo-rey Pri Ha-ga-fen. Amen.

All together:

Blessed are You, Lord our God, King of the universe, who creates the fruit of the vine. Amen.

(All drink.)

All together:

Yeshua, break these chains that tie me to the bondage of this world.

RACHTZAH: WASHING HANDS BEFORE THE MEAL

All together:

Ba-ruch At-ah Adonai E-lo-hei-nu Me-lech Ha-olam, A-sher Kid-sha-nu B'mitz-vo-tav v'tzi-va-nu

An-na-tie-lat Yah-da-yim.

All together:

Blessed are you, O Lord our God, King of the universe, who has sanctified us with His commandments, and has commanded the washing of our hands.

MOTZI: PRAYERS BEFORE THE MEAL

The Hebrew word for "bread" is *lechem*. It also means "to battle." A meal is like a war between that which is material and that which is spiritual. This is why we pray over our food.

All together:

Ba-ruch At-ah Adonai E-lo-hei-nu Me-lech Ha-olam, Ha-mo-tsi Lechem Min Ha'aretz. Amen.

All together:

Blessed are You, Lord our God, King of the universe, who brings forth bread from the earth. Amen.

MATZAH: BLESSING OVER UNLEAVENED BREAD

Matzah emphasizes the power of selflessness. By eating matzah, the food of humility, we assume its qualities.

All together:

Ba-ruch At-ah Adonai E-lo-hei-nu Me-lech Ha-olam,

A-sher Kid-sha-nu B'mitz-vo-tav V'tzi-va-nu Al Akhi-lat

Matzah. Amen.

All together:

Blessed are You, Lord our God, King of the universe, who has sanctified us through his commandments, and commanded us to eat unleavened bread. Amen.

MAROR: BLESSING OVER BITTER HERBS

Bitter herbs teach us the process of growth. An olive does not produce oil until it is pressed. So too, *maror*, bitterness, hardens our mettle. It is the setbacks and pain in life that strengthen us.

All together:

Ba-ruch At-ah Adonai E-lo-hei-nu Me-lech Ha-olam,

A-sher Kid-sha-nu B'mitz-vo-tavv'tzi-va-nu Al Akhi-lat.

Amen.

All together:

Blessed are You Lord our God, King of the universe, who has sanctified us through his commandments and commanded us to eat bitter herbs. Amen.

KORECH: MAKE A MATZAH SANDWICH

Take a piece of matzah and break it in half. Create a sandwich by putting the horseradish and charoset on the matzah and eat it.

Shulchan Orech: Time to Eat!

Luke 22:20 (HNV): He took the cup in like manner after supper, saying, "This cup is the new covenant in my blood, that which is poured out for you."

Exodus 6:6b (HNV): "I will redeem You with an outstretched arm, and with great judgments."

BAREKH: BLESSING AFTER THE MEAL

THIRD CUP: THE CUP OF REDEMPTION

Stand for the blessing:

All together:

Ba-ruch At-ah Adonai E-lo-hei-nu Me-lech Ha-olam, Bo-rey Pri Ha-ga-fen. Amen

All together:

Blessed are You, Lord our God, King of the universe, who creates the fruit of the vine. Amen.

(All drink.)

All together:

Yeshua, Thank You for redeeming me with Your outstretched arms.

Job 19:25–26 (HNV): But as for me, I know that my Redeemer lives. In the end, he will stand upon the [earth]. After my skin is destroyed, then in my flesh shall I see God.

TZAFUN: "HIDDEN"

Leader:

Have the children seek until they find the afikomen (middle matzah). After it is found, break it up into small pieces and have everyone at the table eat a piece. This represents the bread of life, Yeshua, who has been resurrected, and we are to partake in Him. *Afikomen* means "that which comes after," as in Messiah's return! Therefore, the afikomen is thought of as dessert. How sweet will that Day be?

Matthew 26:30 (HNV): When they had sung [the Hallel], they went out to the Mount of Olives.

Psalm 118:22–24 (HNV): The stone which the builders rejected has become the head of the corner. This is the LORD's doing. It is marvelous in our eyes. This is the day that the LORD has made. We will rejoice and be glad in it!

John 19:19 (HNV): Pilate wrote a title also, and put it on the cross. There was written, "YESHUA OF [NAZARETH], THE KING OF THE [JEWS]."

Matthew 2:22–23 (HNV): Being warned in a dream, he withdrew into the region of [Galilee], and came and lived in a city called [Nazareth]; that it might be fulfilled which was spoken through the prophets: "He will be called a [Nazarene]."

Zechariah 3:8 (HNV): Hear now, [Joshua the high priest], you and your fellows who sit before you; for they are men who are a sign: for, behold, I will bring forth my servant, the Branch.

Zechariah 6:11–12 (HNV): "Yes, take silver and gold, and make crowns, and set them on the head of [Joshua] the son of [Jehozadak], the [high priest]; and speak to him, saying, 'Thus says the LORD of Hosts, 'Behold, the man whose name is the Branch.'"

John 19:5 (HNV): Yeshua therefore came out, wearing the crown of thorns and the purple garment. Pilate said to them, "Behold, the man!"

Psalm 49:6–9 (HNV): Those who trust in their wealth, and boast in the multitude of their riches—none of them can by any means redeem his brother, nor give God a ransom for him. For the redemption of their life is costly, no payment is ever enough, that he should live on forever, that he should not see corruption.

Isaiah 53:3–5 (HNV): He was despised, and rejected by men; a man of suffering, and acquainted with grief: and as one from whom men hide their face he was despised; and we didn't respect him. Surely he has borne our infirmities, and carried our sorrows; yet we esteemed him stricken, struck of

God, and afflicted. But he was wounded for our transgressions, he was bruised for our iniquities; the chastisement of our shalom was on him; and with his stripes we are healed.

Isaiah 53:6–10 (HNV): All we like sheep have gone astray; we have turned everyone to his own way; and the LORD has laid on him the iniquity of us all. He was oppressed, yet when he was afflicted he didn't open his mouth; as a lamb that is led to the slaughter, and as a sheep that before its shearers is mute, so he didn't open his mouth. By oppression and judgment he was taken away; and as for his generation, who [among them] considered that he was cut off out of the land of the living and disobedience of my people to whom the stroke [was due]? They made his grave with the wicked, and with a rich man in his death; although he had done no violence, neither was any deceit in his mouth.

Matthew 27:27–29 (HNV): Then the governor's soldiers took Yeshua into the Praetorium, and gathered to him the whole cohort. They stripped him, and put a scarlet robe on him. They braided a crown of thorns and put it on his head, and a reed in his right hand; and they kneeled down before him, and mocked him, saying, "Hail, King of the [Jews]!"

Matthew 27:30–31 (ESV): And they spit on him and took the reed and struck him on the head. And when they had mocked him, they stripped him of the robe and put his own clothes on him and led him away to crucify him.

Mark 15:21–25 (HNV): They compelled one passing by, coming from the country, [Simon] of Cyrene, the father of Alexander and Rufus, to go with them, that he might bear his cross. They brought him to the place called [Golgotha], which is, being interpreted, "The place of a skull." They offered him wine mixed with myrrh to drink, but he didn't take it. Crucifying him, they parted his garments among them, casting lots on them, what each should take. It was the third hour, and they crucified him.

Psalm 118:27 (HNV): The LORD is God, and he has given us light. Bind the sacrifice with cords, even to the horns of the altar.

Matthew 27:45–47 (HNV): Now from the sixth hour there was darkness over all the land until the ninth hour. About the ninth hour Yeshua cried with a loud voice, saying, "Eli, Eli, lama [sabachthani]?" That is, "My God, my God, why have you forsaken me?" Some of them who stood there, when they heard it, said, "This man calls [Elijah]."

Psalm 118:16 (HNV): "The right hand of the LORD is exalted! The right hand of the LORD does valiantly!"

Matthew 27:50–51 (HNV): Yeshua cried again with a loud voice, and yielded up his spirit. Behold, the veil of the temple was torn in two from the top to the bottom. The [earth] quaked and the rocks were split.

KERIAH: "TEARING"
(Mourning Ritual)

Tearing a garment was an ancient custom for those in mourning over close relatives to express their grief in biblical times.

The veil of Temple is the Father's garment!

Jeremiah 32:17–21 (HNV): Ah Lord GOD! Behold, you have made the heavens and the [earth] by your great power and by your outstretched arm; there is nothing too hard for you, who show lovingkindness to thousands, and recompense the iniquity of the fathers into the bosom of their children after them; the great, the mighty God, the LORD of Hosts is his name; great in counsel, and mighty in work; whose eyes are open on all the ways of the sons of men, to give everyone according to his ways, and according to the fruit of his doings: who performed signs and wonders in the land of [Egypt], even to this day, both in [Israel] and among [other] men; and mad[e] you a name, as in this day; and did bring forth your people [Israel] out of the land of [Egypt] with signs, and with wonders, and with a strong hand, and with an outstretched arm, and with great terror.

Zechariah 12:9–10 (ESV): "And on that day I will seek to destroy all the nations that come against Jerusalem. And I will pour out on the house of David and the inhabitants of Jerusalem a spirit of grace and pleas for mercy, so that, when they look on me, on him whom they have pierced, they shall mourn for him, as one mourns for an only child, and weep bitterly over him, as one weeps over a firstborn."

John 20:27–28 (ESV): Then he said to Thomas, "Put your finger here, and see my hands; and put out your hand, and place it in my side. Do not disbelieve, but believe." Thomas answered him, "My Lord and my God!"

HALLEL: SONGS OF PRAISE
Stand for blessing.

All together:

Psalm 113:1–9 (HNV): Praise the LORD! Praise, you servants of the LORD, praise the name of the LORD. Blessed be the name of the LORD, from this time forth and forevermore. From the rising of the sun to the going down of the same, The LORD's name is to be praised. The LORD is high above all nations, his glory above the heavens. Who is like the LORD, our God, who has his seat on high, who stoops down to see in heaven and in the [earth]? He raises up the poor out of the dust. Lifts up the needy from the ash heap; that he may set him with princes, even with the princes of his people. He settles the barren woman in her home, as a joyful mother of children. Praise the LORD!

Psalm 114:1–8 (HNV): When [Israel] went forth out of [Egypt], the house of [Jacob] from a people of foreign language; [Judah] became his sanctuary, [Israel] his dominion. The sea saw it, and fled. The [Jordan] was driven back. The mountains skipped like rams, the little hills like lambs. What was it, you sea, that you fled? You [Jordan], that you turned back? You mountains, that you skipped like rams; you little hills, like lambs? Tremble, you [earth], at the presence of the Lord, at the presence of the God of [Jacob], who turned the rock into a pool of water, the flint into a spring of waters.

Psalm 115:1–3 (HNV): Not to us, LORD, not to us, but to your name give glory, for your lovingkindness, and for your truth's sake. Why should the nations say, "Where is their

God, now?" But our God is in the heavens. He does whatever he pleases.

Psalm 116:12–13 (HNV): What will I give to the LORD for all his benefits toward me? I will take the cup of salvation, and call on the name of the LORD.

Psalm 117:1–2 (HNV): Praise the LORD, all you nations! Extol him, all you peoples! For his lovingkindness is great toward us. The LORD's faithfulness endures forever. Praise the LORD!

Psalm 118:5–8 (HNV): Out of my distress, I called on the LORD. The LORD answered me with freedom. The LORD is on my side. I will not be afraid. What can man do to me? The LORD is on my side among those who help me. Therefore I will look in triumph at those who hate me. It is better to take refuge in the LORD, than to put confidence in man.

NIRTZAH: "ACCEPTED"

Ephesians 1:6–7 (ESV): To the praise of his glorious grace, with which he has blessed us in the Beloved. In him we have redemption through his blood, the forgiveness of our trespasses, according to the riches of his grace.

FOURTH CUP: CUP OF ACCEPTANCE

Stand for blessing:

All together:

Ba-ruch At-ah Adonai E-lo-hei-nu Me-lech Ha-olam,

Bo-rey Pri Ha-ga-fen. Amen.

All together:

Blessed are You, Lord our God, King of the universe, who creates the fruit of the vine. Amen.

(All drink.)

All together:

Yeshua, thank You for accepting me into Your family. I accept You now into my heart.

FIFTH CUP: CUP OF ELIJAH

Malachi 4:4–6 (HNV): "Remember the law of Moses my servant, which I commanded to him in Horev for all Yisra'el, even statutes and ordinances. Behold, I will send you Eliyah the prophet before the great and terrible day of the LORD comes. He will turn the hearts of the fathers to the children, and the hearts of the children to their fathers, lest I come and strike the eretz with a curse."

Stand for blessing.

All together:

Ba-ruch At-ah Adonai E-lo-hei-nu Me-lech Ha-olam,
Bo-rey Pri Ha-ga-fen. Amen.

All together:

Blessed are You, Lord our God, King of the universe, who creates the fruit of the vine. Amen.

(All drink.)

L'SHANA HABA'AH BE'YERUSHALAYIM NEXT YEAR IN JERUSALM! We Want Messiah Now!

CLOSE WITH PRIESTLY BLESSING
Leader/Father:

> **Numbers 6:24–27 (ESV):** The LORD bless you and keep you; the LORD make his face to shine upon you and be gracious to you; the LORD lift up his countenance upon you and give you peace. "So shall they put my name upon the people of Israel, and I will bless them."

HOW TO SET THE TABLE
Since Seder is a feast, or special occasion, we suggest using a nice tablecloth, napkins, flatware, and glasses.

Each place setting should have its own glass for wine or grape juice as well as a paper napkin for the rehearsing of the plagues. We also suggest each person have his or her own Haggadah for the blessings.

At the center of the table, place:

- the Seder tray with the shank bone, bitter herbs, charoset, roasted egg, horseradish, and parsley

- a small dish with salt water within easy reach (more than one dish might be needed)

- a bottle of wine or grape juice

- an empty wine glass for the Cup of Elijah

- at least three pieces of Afikomen, covered

- basin, cup, and towel for washing of hands

GLOSSARY OF TERMS

Hebrew	English
Pesach	Passover
Chametz	leaven, yeast
Charoset	clay
Beitzah	roasted egg
Karpas	vegetable
Maror	bitter herb
Matzo	unleavened bread
Yachatz	to break
Tzafun	hidden

Greek	English
Afikomen	that which comes after

Purge out the old yeast, that you may be a new lump, even as you are unleavened. For indeed Messiah, our [Passover], has been sacrificed in our place.

—1 Corinthians 5:7 (HNV)

The Old is in the New contained.

The New is in the Old explained.

The Old is in the New concealed.

The New is in the Old revealed.

FUTURE DATES FOR PASSOVER/UNLEAVENED BREAD

YEAR	PESACH	UNLEAVENED BREAD
2017	April 10	April 11
2018	March 30	March 31
2019	April 19	April 20
2020	April 8	April 9
2021	March 27	March 28
2022	April 15	April 16
2023	April 5	April 6
2024	April 22	April 23

WHAT IS PASSOVER?

Passover is the fourteenth day of the month of Nisan. It is celebrated in Jewish homes with a Seder. The story of Passover is often recounted during the Seder and read from a Haggadah.

Traditionally symbolic foods, like charoset and horseradish, are eaten. The symbolic foods are placed on a specific plate called a Seder plate/tray. No leavened foods are eaten during Passover.

The Passover Seder is an annual reminder to the families about their ancestors suffering in Egypt and of the miraculous deliverance from their bondage.

Follow along and you will see how the Lord has it all planned out! Come and join us as we dive deeper into our Jewish roots and discover so much more than what is on the surface! The Lord wants you to find Him in His Torah, His Word, which is dear to His heart. As you know, out of the abundance of the heart, the mouth speaks; and the Torah was just that! The spoken Word of God, directly from His mouth and heart, for all of humankind to learn from.

APPENDIX 2

EREV SHABBAT:

A BELIEVER'S GUIDE FOR THE EVENING

SABBATH MEAL, BY SUSIE MCELROY*

Then God blessed the seventh day and sanctified it, because in it He rested from all His work which God had created and made.

—Genesis 2:3

"And it shall be from new moon to new moon and from sabbath to sabbath, all mankind will come to bow down before Me," says the LORD.

—Isaiah 66:23

INTRODUCTION

Living in the prophetic times that we are living in, a lot of believers are being called back to the Hebrew roots of their faith, causing a desire for us to learn about the Sabbath. The Sabbath

---

*Scriptures in appendix 2 are from the NASB.

is God's first appointed time He set aside for us to connect with Him in a special way. The Sabbath is from sunset Friday to sunset Saturday. This booklet is designed to help guide your family and friends through the beauty and joy of the weekly Friday evening Sabbath meal. It is purposely written to be easy to follow, short, and simple, giving you the confidence to host a Sabbath meal. We have found over many years of hosting Sabbath dinners that most people love experiencing them. We pray that you will be encouraged to take time to have Sabbath dinner, to connect with God, family, and friends as never before and to find rest for your souls in our Master Yeshua HaMashiach. Shabbat shalom,

—SUSIE MCELROY

THE FEAST OF SHABBAT

The Sabbath truly is a feast for all mankind, as Yeshua even declared it was made just for us! It is to be a time set apart just for you and God. Look what is offered you:

> "If because of the sabbath, you turn your foot from doing your own pleasure on My holy day, and call the sabbath a delight, the holy day of the LORD honorable, and honor it, desisting from your own ways, from seeking your own pleasure and speaking your own word, then you will take delight in the LORD, and I will make you ride on the heights of the earth; and I will feed you with the heritage of Jacob your father, for the mouth of the LORD has spoken."

—Isaiah 58:13–14

The Sabbath is the first feast of the Lord mentioned in Leviticus 23. This word, *feast*, means an appointed time for God to meet with you. Who in their right minds would want to turn that appointment down? The Sabbath is for everyone who wants to be in covenant with God. Look at what else Isaiah says:

> Also the foreigners who join themselves to the LORD, to minister to Him, and to love the name of the LORD, to be His servants, every one who keeps from profaning the sabbath and holds fast My covenant; even those I will bring to My holy mountain and make them joyful in My house of prayer.

—Isaiah 56:6–7a

Take hold of the Sabbath of the Lord and enter His covenant, and watch Him take hold of you.

—Pastor Mark Biltz, El Shaddai Ministries

SETTING THE SABBATH TABLE

If possible, use dishes and table linens that are set apart for your Sabbath table or other special times of celebration.

- Set your table with a white tablecloth and napkins or place mats of your choice.

- Place two candleholders with white candles or tea lights in the center of your table. You may add an additional candle or tea light for each woman present.

- Place a bottle of wine and/or grape juice on the table, and set a wine glass at each place setting.

- Place two loaves of challah on the table, covering them with a white cloth or challah cover.

- Place a small bowl of salt on the table for dipping the challah.

- Place a bowl of water and a hand towel on the table next to the father or leader.

- Place a copy of this Erev Shabbat Guide next to each place setting.

MOTHER'S PRAYER TO USHER IN THE SABBATH

Sabbath begins on Friday evening at sunset. If you have a shofar, your family and friends might enjoy blowing it to welcome the Sabbath. Children find this especially fun. The mother or woman of the house prays this prayer before sunset. If no woman is present, a man may pray this.

May the Sabbath lights bring into our home the beauty of truth and the radiance of God's love.

May the Lord bless us with His Sabbath joy.

May the Lord bless us with His Sabbath holiness.

May the Lord bless us with His Sabbath peace.

Amen.

CANDLE-LIGHTING BLESSING

The mother or woman of the house lights two candles, one to remember the Sabbath and one to observe it. She may cover her head as a reminder that God is her covering. She lights the candles and invites each woman present to light a candle or tea light.

All the women recite this blessing together after they light the candles:

Ba-rukh at-tah Adonai E-lo-he-nu me-lekh

Ha-o-lam a-sher kid-de-sha-nu b'mitz-vo-tav

v'tzi-va-nu le-hi-yot ohr la-goy-im

ve-na-tan-la-nu et Ye-shu-a me-shi-chei-nu ohr ha-o-lam

Blessed are You, Lord our God, King of the universe, who sanctifies us with His commandments and commanded us to be a light to the nations and who gave to us Yeshua our Messiah, the Light of the World.

Amen.

A HUSBAND'S BLESSING FOR HIS WIFE

Married couples face each other and husbands quietly say this blessing from Proverbs 31 over their wives. Single men at the table are also encouraged to say this blessing as a reminder that they are the bride of Messiah.

An excellent wife, who can find?

You are far more precious than jewels.

My heart trusts in you and you enrich my life.

You bring me good, not harm, all the days of your life.

You extend a helping hand to the poor

and open your arms to the needy.

Strength and dignity are your clothing

and you smile without fear at the future.

You speak with wisdom, and the teaching

of kindness is on your tongue.

You look well to the ways of our household

and do not eat the bread of idleness.

Our children rise up and call you blessed

and I do also.

Many women have done excellently,

but you surpass them all.

Charm is deceitful and beauty is fleeting,

but because you fear the Lord, you shall be praised.

I honor you for all that you have done,

your works will bring you praise.

A WIFE'S BLESSING FOR HER HUSBAND

Still facing each other, wives quietly say this blessing from Psalm 1 over their husbands. Single women at the table are encouraged to also say this blessing as a reminder that they are the bride of Messiah.

> Blessed are you [HUSBAND'S NAME], because you do not walk in the counsel of the ungodly, nor stand in the way of sinners, nor sit in the seat of mockers. But your delight is in the Law of the LORD, and in His Law do you meditate day and night. You shall be like a tree firmly planted by rivers of water, which yields its fruit in season, whose leaf does not wither, and whatever you do shall prosper.

BLESSING OVER SONS

The father lays his hands on the head of each of his sons present and prays this blessing over them. You may also want to pray a personal blessing over each child.

> For sons pray:

> The Lord bless you with the blessing of Ephraim and Manasseh. May you forget the pain of your past and be fruitful every day of your life. May the Lord make you a good husband and father and prepare a holy wife for you.

> (based on Genesis 48:20)

BLESSING OVER DAUGHTERS

> For daughters pray:

The Lord bless you to be like Sarah, Rebekah, Rachel, and Leah. May He clothe you with virtue and compassion. May the Lord grant you long life. May the Lord bring you a husband who will care for you, protect you, and defend you. May He favor you with happiness and peace.

(based on Ruth 4:11)

AARONIC BLESSING
Blessing Guests

The father or leader stands to pray this blessing from Numbers 6:24–26 over all the guests at the table.

Father/Leader:

> Y'-va-re-ch'-cha Adonai v'yish-m'-re-cha ya-er Adonai pa-nav a le-cha vi-chu-ne-ka yi-sa Adonai pa-nav a-le-cha v'ya-sem l'-cha shalom

The Lord bless you, and keep you;

The Lord make His face shine on you, and be gracious to you;

The Lord lift up His countenance on you, and give you peace.

PRAYER FOR ISRAEL

This prayer was written by the chief rabbi of the State of Israel in 1948. It is prayed in synagogues all over the world each Shabbat (based on Deuteronomy 30:4–5).

Together:

Our Father in Heaven, Protector and Redeemer of Israel, bless the State of Israel which marks the first glimmering of our deliverance. Shield it beneath the wings of Your love; spread over it Your canopy of peace; send Your light and Your truth to its leaders, officers and counselors, and direct them with Your good counsel. O God, strengthen the defenders of our Holy Land; grant them salvation and crown them with victory. Establish peace in the land and everlasting joy for its inhabitants. Remember our brethren, the whole house of Israel, in all the lands of their dispersion.

Speedily let them walk upright to Zion, the city, to Jerusalem, Your dwelling place, as it is written in the Torah of Your servant Moses, "Even if you are dispersed in the uttermost parts of the world, from there the LORD your God will gather and fetch you. The LORD your God will bring you into the land which your fathers possessed, and you shall possess it." Unite our hearts to love and revere Your Name, and to observe all the precepts of Your Torah. Shine forth in Your glorious majesty over all the inhabitants of Your world. Let everything that breathes proclaim, "The LORD God of Israel is King; His majesty rules over all." Amen.

BLESSING OVER WINE (KIDDUSH / SANCTIFICATION)

Wine is a symbol of joy in Psalm 104. The Sabbath is to be a joy. We lift our glasses and say this blessing together. Then we can toast to our health in Hebrew saying, "L'Chaim" (To life!).

Together:

ba-ruch at-tah Adonai E-lo-he-nu

me-lekh ha-o-lam bo-rei p'ri ha-ga-fen

Blessed are You, Lord our God, King of the universe,

Creator of the fruit of the vine. Amen.

L'Chaim

HAND WASHING

The father or leader takes the bowl and towel around the table, serving each guest, beginning with his wife. Each guest dips his or her right hand, then his or her left hand in the water and dries them on the towel. After everyone is finished, the wife or first guest served holds the bowl and towel for her husband or leader.

Father/Leader:

We wash our hands as a visual reminder that Yeshua has washed us clean by His blood and given us the Living Waters of the Holy Spirit. Wash hands now.

Together:

> Blessed are You, Lord our God, King of the universe,
>
> who has washed us clean
>
> by the power of the Holy Spirit
>
> and the completed work of Messiah Yeshua
>
> and has called us to be set apart
>
> for His kingdom and glory. Amen.
>
> (See Psalm 24:3–4.)

BLESSING OVER BREAD HA-MOTZI

The challah is passed around the table. Each guest tears off a small piece and dips it in salt. Then everyone eats the bread together. Salt represents an everlasting covenant before the Lord. (See Numbers 18:19.)

Together:

> Ba-ruch at-tah Adonai
>
> E-lo-he-nu me-lekh ha-o-lam
>
> ha-mo-tzi Yeshua ha-le-chem ha-chai min ha-E'retz
>
> Blessed are you, Lord our God,
>
> King of the universe,

who brings forth Yeshua, the Living Bread

from the earth.

Amen.

(See John 6:35.)

Time to enjoy your Sabbath meal.

BLESSING AFTER MEAL

When you have eaten and are satisfied, you shall bless the LORD your God for the good land which He has given you.
(See Deuteronomy 8:10.)

Together:

Blessed are You, Lord our God, King of the universe, who nourishes the whole world in goodness, with grace, kindness, and compassion.

He gives bread to all flesh, for His mercy endures forever.

And through His great goodness we have never lacked, nor will we lack food forever, for the sake of His great Name.

For He is God, who nourishes and sustains all, and does good to all, and prepares food for all His creatures which He created.

Blessed are You, Lord, who nourishes all.

Amen.

CHALLAH RECIPE
Ingredients:

1 cup warm milk

1/4 to 1/2 cup granulated sugar

1 tablespoon honey

2 eggs (room temperature)

1/2 cup butter, butter-flavored shortening, or coconut oil

2 1/2 teaspoons kosher salt

4 cups flour (all-purpose, bread, whole wheat, spelt, or combination of flours)

2 1/4 teaspoons or 1 package active dry yeast

sesame seeds (optional)

Bread Machine Directions:
Place warm milk, sugar, honey, eggs, butter or oil, salt, flour, and yeast in the bread pan (wet ingredients on the bottom, dry ingredients on top). Select the dough cycle. Press start.

After the machine cycle is done, take the dough out and place it on a very lightly floured surface and let rise for 5 minutes.

Hand Kneading or Stand Mixer Directions:
Place warm milk, sugar, honey, and yeast in a large mixing bowl. Let stand for 5 minutes or until yeast starts to activate. Add eggs and butter or oil and mix until blended. Add 2 cups flour and mix well. Slowly add the remainder of the flour, mixing well. Knead by hand or machine for 6 to 8 minutes until smooth, adding a

little more flour if needed so it does not stick to the bowl.

Take the dough out and place it on a lightly floured surface and let rise for 5 minutes.

Place the dough in front of you before it has been formed into any shape. Recite the following blessing.

Blessing
Blessed are You, Lord our God, King of the universe, who has sanctified us with His commandments, and inspired us to separate the challah.

Remove a small piece from the dough, lift it and say:
This is challah.

Burn the separated dough or wrap it in two layers (e.g., a napkin) and discard it.

Baking Directions:
Divide the dough in half. Then divide each half into 3 equal pieces. Roll each piece into ropes about 12 to 14 inches long and braid into two loaves.

Gently put the loaves on parchment paper, cover with a clean towel, and let rise for 1 to 1 1/2 hours in a warm, draft-free place until double in size.

Preheat oven to 350 degrees. In a small bowl, beat together 1 egg and 1 tablespoon of water. Brush risen loaves with egg mixture. Sprinkle with sesame seeds.

Bake in preheated oven for about 20 to 25 minutes. If the bread begins to brown too soon, cover the loaves with foil.

The dough or baked challah freezes well. Challah also makes great French toast on Shabbat morning.

UNLEAVENED ALMOND ROCA

4 1/2 to 5 whole matzos

1 1/2 cup butter

1 1/2 cup brown sugar

12 ounces chocolate chips

1 cup sliced almonds

Preheat the oven to 350 degrees.

Cover a cookie sheet with matzo. Begin by layering 2 whole matzos, and then break the others to fill in the remaining space on cookie sheet.

Combine the butter and brown sugar in a heavy saucepan. Bring to a boil over medium-high heat and boil for about 5 minutes.

Pour the butter mixture evenly over the matzo and bake in the oven for about 5 minutes, until bubbly.

Remove from the oven and sprinkle with chocolate chips. Return to the oven and cook until the chocolate chips are glossy and spreadable (about 1 minute). Remove from the oven and spread the chocolate evenly over the top.

Press the almonds into the chocolate. Cut into desired portions while still warm, placing on wax or parchment paper to cool.

Michelle Schneberger, El Shaddai Ministries

RECOMMENDED JEWISH WORKS

The Jewish Holy Days: Their Spiritual Significance
Moshe Braun, Aronson Publishing, © 1996, ISBN
1-56821-5533-3

The Jewish Festivals: History and Observance
Hayyim Schauss, Schocken Books, © 1938, ISBN
0-8052-0413-X

*The Jewish Festivals: From Their Beginnings to Our Own
Day*
Hayyim Schauss, UAHC, © 1938

The Jewish Holidays, A Journey through History
Larry Domnitch, Aronson Publishing, © 2000, ISBN
0-7657-6109-2

The Art of Jewish Living: The Passover Seder
Dr. Ron Wolfson, FJMC, © 1988, ISBN 0-935665-01-7

Jewish Holidays and Festivals
Dr. Isidor Margolis and Rabbi Sidney L. Markowitz,
Citadel Press, © 1995, ISBN 0-8065-0285-1

Days of Awe: A Treasury of Traditions, Legends
S. Y. Agnon, Schocken Books, © 1948, ISBN
0-8052-0100-9

*On Wings of Awe: A Machzor for Rosh Hashanah and Yom
Kippur*
B'Nai B'rith Hillel Foundation, © 1985

Rosh Hashanah Yom Kippur Survival Kit
Shimon Apisdorf, Leviathan Press, © 2000, ISBN
1-881927-14-8

The Rosh Hashanah Anthology
Philip Goodman, Jewish Publication Society, © 1970,
ISBN 0-8276-0408-4

The Passover Anthology
Philip Goodman, Jewish Publication Society, © 1961

Ramban Haggadah
Artscroll, © 1996, ISBN 0-89906-390-X

The Sabbath
Abraham Joshua Heschel, Farrar, Straus and Giroux, ©
1951

CHRISTIAN/MESSIANIC WORKS

The Feasts of the Lord: God's Prophetic Calendar from Calvary to the Kingdom
Kevin Howard and Marvin Rosenthal, Thomas Nelson Publishing, © 1997, ISBN 0-7852-7518-5

The Seven Festivals of the Messiah
Edward Chumney, Treasure House, © 1994, ISBN 1-56043-767-7

The Fall Feasts of Israel
Mitch and Zhava Glaser, Moody Press, © 1987, ISBN 0-8024-2539-9

The Feasts of Adonai: Why Christians Should Look at the Biblical Feasts
Valerie Moody, © 2009

Celebrate the Feasts of the Old Testament in Your Own Home or Church
Martha Zimmerman, Bethany House, © 1981, ISBN 0-87123-228-6

Celebrate the Feasts of the Lord: The Christian Heritage of the Sacred Jewish Festivals
William Francis, Crest Books, © 1997, ISBN 0-9657601-2-X

Israel's Holy Days in Type and Prophecy
Daniel Fuchs, Loizeaux Brothers, © 1985, ISBN 0-87213-198-X

God's Prophetic Calendar
Lehman Strauss, Loizeaux Brothers, ©1987, ISBN 0-87213-816-X

Rosh HaShanah and the Messianic Kingdom to Come
Joseph Good, Hatikvah Ministries, © 1989

Hanukkah in the Home of the Redeemed, 3rd ed.
Ariel and D'vorah Berkowitz, Shoreshim, © 2005, 978–0975291498

The Spirit of Pentecost
Zola Levitt, Zola Levitt Ministries, © 1978, ISBN 1-930749-16-3

ACKNOWLEDGEMENTS

I'm extremely grateful to all the people at El Shaddai Ministries who made this book possible. All those who attend locally as well as the thousands from around the world who live-stream our services have given me the motivation and encouragement to finish this project. I also need to make special mention of the board at El Shaddai Ministries in their united vision in taking Torah to the nations. Bill Voiss provided totally unwavering support and encouragement with his selfless giving of his time to make sure the ministry runs smoothly while I took time to write. Peter Thalhofer gives his time and wisdom to help us make all the important decisions for fueling our growth. Tina Fallstead, the most dedicated assistant one could have, keeps me focused and on task, solving problems before they happen. Thank you all for your support!

NOTES

CHAPTER 1: THE BIBLICAL CALENDAR

1. Bet Emet Ministries, "Constantine's Easter Letter and the Loss of the Faith Once Given to the Saints," PaulProblem.com, accessed February 23, 2016, http://paulproblem.faithweb.com/constantine_easter_letter.htm; emphasis added.

2. "It's certain that Jesus was not a Jew." Adolf Hitler, in *Hitler's Table Talk 1941–1944: Secret Conversations*, ed. Norman Cameron et al. (New York: Enigma, 2007), 76.

3. Strong's Exhaustive Concordance: New American Standard Bible. 1995. Updated ed. La Habra: Lockman Foundation. http://www.biblestudytools. com/lexicons/hebrew/nas/qara.html.

4. Mishnah (Taanit 4:6); see Numbers 13 for the story.

5. Rosh Hashanah (tractate) 18b.

CHAPTER 2: PASSOVER: THE LAMB SLAIN FROM THE FOUNDATION OF THE WORLD

1. See, for example,www.aish.com http://www.aish.com/jewish-calendar/ and www.hebcal.com http://www.hebcal.com/.

2. Note that in the American King James Version, Exodus 7:10 reads, "and it became a serpent." However, the Hebrew word used there is *tanniyn*, which best describes a crocodile, rather than the snake that we think of when we hear the word *serpent*. See Jeff A. Benner, "Biblical Word of the Month—*Tanniyn*," *Ancient Hebrew Research Center Biblical Hebrew E-Magazine*, February 2013, http://www.ancient-hebrew.org/emagazine/065.pdf.

3. Julius D. W. Staal, *The New Patterns in the Sky: Myths and Legends of the Stars* (n.p.: McDonald and Woodward, 1988).
4. Flavius Josephus, *War of the Jews*, bk. 6, chap. 9.3.
5. Ibid.

CHAPTER 6: ROSH HASHANAH

1. If you want to hear them, check out "Four Traditoinal Jewish Shofar Calls or Blasts," YouTube video, 2:03, posted by James Barbarossa, February 7, 2012, https://www.youtube.com/watch?v=grZDPCKORGg. You can also go to our website and watch the archives of our services, at http://elshaddaiministries. us/.
2. The Hebrew word for her state of sleep here is the same Hebrew word translated in Daniel 12:2 of those who sleep in the dust of the earth.
3. See the 70 Facets website, at http://70facets.org/.

CHAPTER 7: THE FEAST OF YOM KIPPUR

1. On the first day: 13; second day, 12; third day, 11; fourth day, 10; fifth day; 9; sixth day, 8; seventh day, 7; total: 70.
2. Yoma Sukkah 4.5b
3. Josephus, *The War of the* Jew, bk.6, chap. 5.3.293.

CHAPTER 8: THE FEAST OF TABERNACLES

1. Fr. Cassium Folsom, "The Transfiguration and the Feast of Tabernacles (Sukkoth)," Monastero di San Benedetto, March 20, 2011, http://osbnorcia. org/en/2011/03/20/the-transfiguration-and-the-feast-of-tabernacles-sukkoth.
2. Josephus, *War of the Jews*, 6.9.425.
3. Jerusalem Talmud, Sukkah 5.
4. Mishnah, tractate Sukkah 5.
5. Babylonian Talmud Tractate Sukkah.
6. Babylonian Talmud Sukkah 4.
7. Mishnah tractate Sukkah 5:1A-C.
8. Jacob Neusner, *The Babylonian Talmud: A Translation and Commentary*, Mishnah tractate Sotah 9:7–10 (n.p.: Hendrickson, 2005), 309.

INDEX

SCRIPTURE INDEX

13:6–8; 26:17, 74
24:19–20, 127
25:7, 96
258a, 96
25:8b, 96
26:2, 71
26:19, 64
26:20–21, 72
46:10, 5
41:4; 44:6; 48:12, 26
51:6, 103
53:3–5, 177–78
53:6–10, 178
53:9, 39
56:4–7, 129
56:6–7a, 190
58:1, 69
58:13–14, 189
61, 89
61:2, 90
62:5, 77
62:6–7, 77
63:1–2, 91
63:3, 93
63:3–4, 92
66:22, 23, 131
66:23, 188

JEREMIAH
2:8, 110
8:7, 133
17:13, 113–14
27:4–5, 55
30, 74
32:17–21, 180

EZEKIEL
1, 42
3:12, 13, 42
20, 94
20:33–35, 95
24:1–2, 16
33:2–7, 68
38–39, 126
38:19–22, 127
39:17–21, 127
43:1–4, 103
Daniel
2:31–40, 135
3:1–2, 135
6:10, 42
7:2–8, 135
7:9–11, 70
7:24–25, 7
8:3–11, 135
8:13–14, 136
8:16–25, 136
10:1–3, 18
10:5–12, 18
10:13–22, 19
11:31–33, 136
11:32–38, 75
12:1, 62
12:4, 77
12:10, 77

HOSEA
2:19–20, 79
5:15–6:2, 95
6:3, 95
6:4, 95